The Social Engineer's Playbook

A Practical Guide to Pretexting

Jeremiah Talamantes

THE SOCIAL ENGINEER'S PLAYBOOK

A Practical Guide To Pretexting

JEREMIAH TALAMANTES
CISSP, CEH, CHFI, CCISO, CCENT

First Printing: 2014

ISBN-13: 978-0692306611

ISBN-10: 0692306617

Library of Congress Control Number: 2014919212
Hexcode Publishing, Woodbury, MN

Ordering Information:

Special discounts are available on quantity purchases by corporations, associations, educators, and others. For details, contact the publisher at the above listed address.

U.S. trade bookstores and wholesalers: please contact Hexcode Publishing at:
email@hexcodepublishing.com

Dedication

This book is dedicated to my beautiful family. To my precious little girl, Emmy, I hold you in the warmest place in my heart. To my new-born son, Maxwell, I love you so very much little buddy. To my beautiful wife, Katie, I am simply not worthy of you. I love you.

Contents

Acknowledgements

I want to thank my loving parents, Ray and Alma, and my brother Johnnie and his wife, Jenell. I'd also like to thank my father-in-law, Steveo, and my mother-in-law, Beth, for all of their support. Lastly, I'd like to thank RedTeam Security for affording me the opportunity to pursue this endeavor.

RedTeam Security
http://www.redteamsecure.com

http://facebook.com/redteamsecure/

http://twitter.com/redteamsecure/

Preface

This book is about social engineering with a focus on pretexting. Social engineering is not a new concept. There are countless books on various aspects of the subject. My goal in writing this book was to provide an approach toward pretexting that wasn't available when I began my information security career. At the time, there was little published on the topic, let alone material that honed in on pretexting. Therefore, my motivation for writing is to provide additional tactics and insight into pretexting where there is clearly a gap in available information.

My experience with social engineering started many years ago while working as a security consultant. I was fortunate enough to be exposed to the concept before actually performing the work. This helped tremendously to calm my nerves, but I always felt something was missing. While my consulting work had successful results, I felt as if I was repeating the same tactics too often. It seemed as though there wasn't enough creativity or deeper insight into the exploitation of human behavior. My hope is that this book serves to address some of these concerns and sparks social engineers to explore human behaviors through pretexting and exploitation.

Target Audience

This book was written for any person interested in learning more about social engineering with a focus on pretexting. It is assumed, therefore, the reader has a basic working knowledge about social engineering and information technology.

This book is recommended especially for security consultants, IT security analysts, blue teams, red teams, security managers and CISOs. However, if you have an interest in securing your environment or testing other environments, this book is for you.

What This Book Covers

Introduction – introduces the concept of social engineering, its history and different types of social engineering.

Influencing Techniques – discusses several approaches toward influencing and manipulating others. Types of tactics include: reciprocity, authority, scarcity, likability, concession and obligation.

Elicitation – elicitation is a method of gaining intelligence from individuals without them being aware of it. This chapter discusses tactics, such as: flattery, being a sounding board, bracketing, confidential baiting and others.

Pretexting – covers to the psychological manipulation of people into performing actions or divulging confidential information by creating fabricated scenarios.

Information Gathering – discusses the many sources and techniques used to gather valuable intelligence for social engineering purposes.

Tools – provides an overview and guide to using social engineering tools.

The Playbook – includes a varied collection of creative, innovative pretext scenarios to use or augment.

About the Author

Jeremiah Talamantes is the founder of RedTeam Security and the founder and principal security researcher for The Plugbot Project. Jeremiah has nearly 20 years in the IT security industry. He holds a master's degree in information security & assurance and an executive business education from the University of Notre Dame. He is a researcher, author and adjunct faculty member at Norwich University, College of Graduate Studies in information security & assurance. Jeremiah has served as a CISO and expert consultant to several Fortune 500 companies. He is a CISSP, CCISO, CEH, CHFI and CCENT.

Additional Resources:

Research Projects – http://www.redteamsecure.com/labs/all_projects

LinkedIn – http://www.linkedin.com/in/jtalamantes/

Facebook – http://www.facebook.com/redteamsecure

Twitter – http://twitter.com/redteamsecure

Limitation of Liability / Disclaimer of Warranty

THE PUBLISHER AND THE AUTHOR MAKE NO REPRESENTATIONS OR WARRANTIES WITH RESPECT TO THE ACCURACY OF COMPLETENESS OF THE CONTENTS OF THIS WORK AND SPECIFICALLY DISCLAIM ALL WARRANTIES OF FITNESS FOR A PARTICULAR PURPOSE. NO WARRANTY MAY BE CREATED OR EXTENDED BY SALES OR PROMOTIONAL MATERIALS. THE ADVICE AND STRATEGIES CONTAINED HEREIN MAY NOT BE SUITABLE FOR EVERY SITUATION. THIS WORK IS SOLD WITH THE UNDERSTANDING THAT THE PUBLISHER IS NOT ENGAGED IN RENDERING LEGAL, ACCOUNTING OR OTHER PROFESSIONAL SERVICES. NEITHER THE PUBLISHER NOR THE AUTHER SHALL BE LIABLE FOR DAMAGES ARISING HEREFROM. THE FACT THAT AN ORGANIZATION OR WEB SITE IS REFERRED TO IN THIS WORK AS A CITATION, SOURCE OR OTHERWISE DOES NOT MEAN THAT THE AUTHOR OR PUBLISHER ENDORSES THE INFORMATION THE ORGANIZER OF THE WEB SITE MAY PROVIDE OR RECOMMENDATIONS IT MAY MAKE.

Chapter 1: Introduction to Social Engineering

Even within the IT community, many often misinterpret social engineering. This chapter aims to provide a comprehensive introduction to social engineering, its history and some of the concepts that surround it. Many of the tactics and theories discussed in this book may be considered unethical in certain situations. However, the tactics examined here should be used for ethical purposes only.

Social engineering techniques are often thought of as a "dark arts" that only the most elite hackers use or one sees played out in Hollywood movies. I would aim to dispel some of these beliefs by starting out with a comprehensive overview of social engineering.

This chapter will cover the following topics:

- Overview of social engineering
- Brief history of social engineering
- Types of social engineering

Overview

According to Wikipedia, social engineering is defined as "the act of manipulating people into performing actions or divulging confidential information. While similar to a confidence trick or simple fraud, the term typically applies to trickery or deception for the purpose of information gathering, fraud, or computer systems access; in most cases the attacker never comes face-to-face with the victim."

While Wikipedia offers a basic definition of social engineering, I would like to expand on two points. First, the definition of social engineering should be adapted slightly to state that it involves the act of manipulating a person into performing actions that are not in the target's best interest. That is to say, the goal of this book is to provide social engineering techniques to be used in attack scenario simulations where the target (victim) is not in a position of benefitting from the situation. Secondly, the Wikipedia definition also indicates that the attacker almost never comes into physical contact with the victim in real life. This is partly true. A social engineering attack is ordinarily accomplished without face-to-face contact, but the pendulum is beginning to swing in the other direction. Social engineering attacks with some level of physical contact have been rising steadily over the years.

So far we've learned that social engineering attacks are directed at people in an effort to get them to do something beneficial to the attacker such as, getting victims to divulge passwords and credit card information. But the question is, how is this primarily accomplished? The definitive answer to this question is through the manipulation of the human element – trust.

It can easily be said that social engineering is the exploitation of human behavior and trust. After all, convincing or enticing people to do things such as divulging their passwords and other sensitive information is not so straightforward as one might think. Persuading people to give up this kind of information often involves not only planning, deceptiveness and a deep understanding of the factors of human psychological behaviors. It's no wonder that most victims feel attacked on a very personal level.

Social engineers prey on the human intrinsic traits of people wanting to be helpful and wanting to be liked. They understand these traits at a deeper level and craft their attacks accordingly. It is a plan of attack that involves playing on human emotion, deceptive tricks and lies and the service industry is often smack dab in the crosshairs. After all, what better industries to exploit than those that are supposed to be helpful and courteous? This is especially true in the Hospitality industry. But does it mean that service people should be defensive and rude? Absolutely not. It does, however, call for is a change in behavior and the wherewithal to know when you're under attack and what to do about it.

Before digging deeper into the specifics of social engineering tactics, let's take a look at the history of social engineering.

History

Some believe social engineering began as a result of recent technological advances, such as email spear phishing. The practice, however, has been around for ages in a number of different forms. It has merely evolved over the years.

Photo of Charles Ponzi – famous con artist

George Parker is responsible for the popular expression, "And if you believe that, I have a bridge to sell you." Many have used the expression but might no understand exactly where it came from. In the early 1900s, George Parker used social engineering tactics to con tourists into buying famous landmarks, such as the Brooklyn Bridge. Also who could forget Charles Ponzi? In 1920 he was exposed in a massive "Ponzi scheme" to swindle money out of investors with the promises of unbelievable returns.

Kevin Mitnick and Frank Abagnale are two more examples of extraordinary social engineers. who carried out their exploits resulting in theft of proprietary software to masquerading as a Pan Am airline pilot.

One such historic example of social engineering is Ulysses, the leader of the Greek army, who built the infamous Trojan horse that ultimately led to the fall of Troy. During a siege in this historic battle, Ulysses managed to trick the Trojan army into believing his men had given up by leaving a large wooden horse as a sign of retreat just outside of the city's gates. Well, I think we all know how the story played out. How does this story apply today? The Trojan horse strategy might as well be a page torn right out of today's social engineer's playbook. As the old adage goes, "History, with all her volumes vast, hath but one page."

Types of Social Engineering

Unbeknownst to many, there are several types of social engineering attacks. It seems only the most elaborate ones are glamorized in the movies or manage to get press coverage. According to the Verizon Data Breach Report 2012, 37% of all records breached were the result of a social engineering attack. Those attacks weren't the result of some elaborate scheme to take over a nuclear power plant or launch missiles into space. Instead, they involved classic social engineering tactics called, "Pretexting." Pretexting is a common tactic where a social engineer masquerades himself/herself as a person of authority. This usually plays itself out as a social engineer pretending to be a network support person who urgently needs access to the company's server room in order to "fix" something. Or he/she is pretending to be a friend or colleague with an important email attachment for you to see. Using these delivery mechanisms, a social engineer can be very creative with their pretext.

Email (Phishing/Spear phishing)

Phishing is a form of social engineering that is designed to acquire information about someone (username, password, bank information, etc.) while purporting to be someone of authority, such as Facebook or a bank. Phishing emails are designed to look and feel like they're coming from a trusted authority but whose intent is to spread malware or steal data through malicious hyperlinks or HTML forms. Phishing attacks cast a wide net attempting to reel in as many victims as possible, while spear phishing attacks are targeted attacks pointed directly at either a company, industry or even specific people.

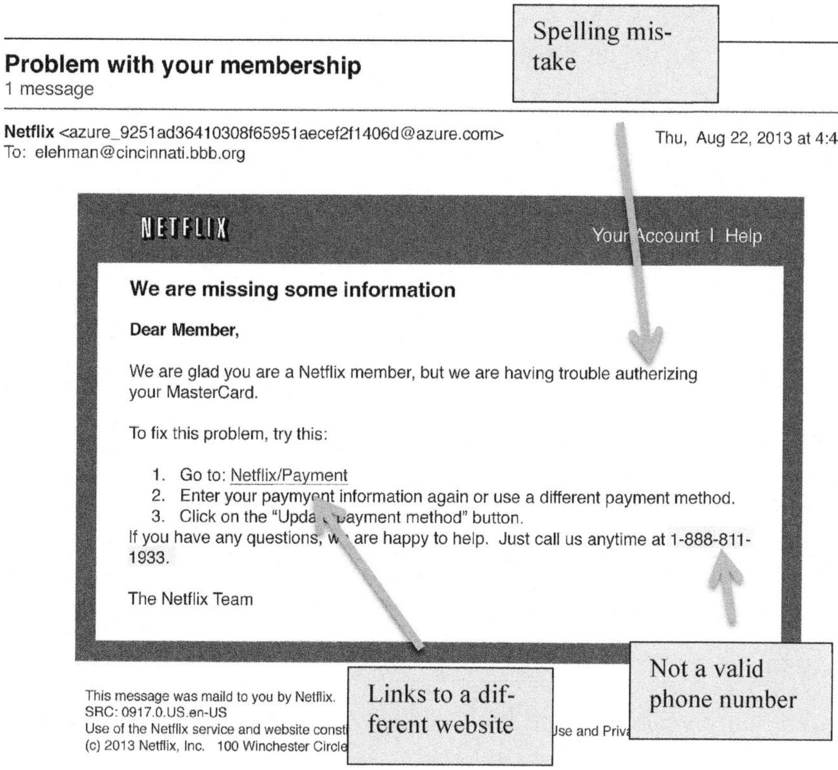

Spelling mistake

Problem with your membership
1 message

Netflix <azure_9251ad36410308f65951aecef2f1406d@azure.com>
To: elehman@cincinnati.bbb.org

Thu, Aug 22, 2013 at 4:44 PM

NETFLIX

Your Account | Help

We are missing some information

Dear Member,

We are glad you are a Netflix member, but we are having trouble autherizing your MasterCard.

To fix this problem, try this:

1. Go to: Netflix/Payment
2. Enter your paymyent information again or use a different payment method.
3. Click on the "Update payment method" button.

If you have any questions, we are happy to help. Just call us anytime at 1-888-811-1933.

The Netflix Team

Not a valid phone number

Links to a different website

This message was maild to you by Netflix.
SRC: 0917.0.US.en-US
Use of the Netflix service and website consti… …Use and Priv…
(c) 2013 Netflix, Inc. 100 Winchester Circle…

An example of a spear phishing email

Telephone (Vishing)

Telephone or voice phishing, also referred to as "vishing," is a social engineering attack conducted over the telephone. This form is used by attackers to steal banking information by purporting to be a representative from their bank's fraud department while asking the victim to validate his or her account by giving credit card information over the phone. In an attack against a business, an attacker often pretends to be help desk support, an executive end users or another position of authority.

This form of social engineering is used quite heavily. According to statistics, those outside of the United States perform this type of social engineering often. This is mostly due to the remote aspect and the perceived safety of not being physically present.

Baiting

Scattering USB drives around a company's front door is a popular form of "baiting" a victim. USB drives labeled with interesting titles ("swimsuit pics" or "payroll") trigger human curiosity. Meanwhile, malicious programs on the USB drive are designed to silently launch and attack once plugged into a computer. A security consultant named Steve Stasuikonis originally made this kind of social engineering popular many years ago and its popularity continues to today.

Fax

Fax? Yes, fax. It's true people still fax documents. In fact, some organizations make heavy use of faxed documents. Many financial organizations exchange requests and authorizations for things such as credit checks and respond back via fax with personally identifiable information. These companies are among the many that face social engineering threats of this type. With the half-duplex, analog nature of facsimile, it becomes rather trivial to spoof fax headers and "become" an organization of authority. All in all, the fax machine breathes on and is expected to be an attack surface going forward.

Pretexting

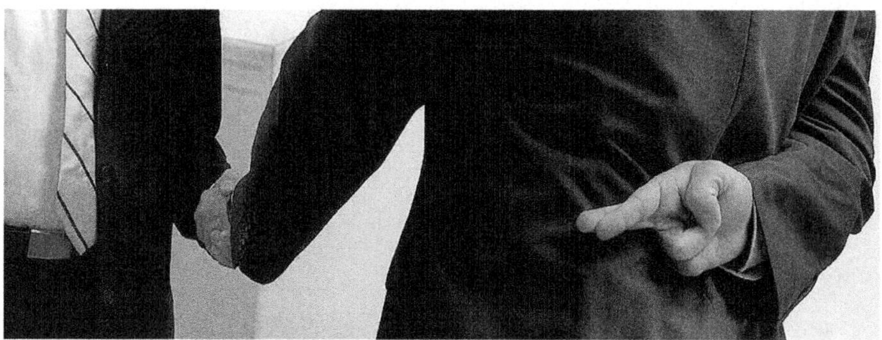

This form of social engineering often involves the attacker confronting the target face to face. Attackers often pretend to be service repair people (IT support or telephone) and use props (disguises, fake work orders or uniforms). They develop fictitious stories about how systems are down and emergency access to the data center is needed. With the anonymity that the Internet provides, one would assume this form of social engineering represents a small percentage of attacks. However, the truth is, it's one of the forms of social engineering that is growing by leaps and bounds.

According to the 2012 Verizon Data Breach Investigation Report, social engineering incidents involving physical tactics made up 37 percent of all social engineering attacks. This metric is second only to telephone social engineering incidents, while noting a marked increase in these attacks from 2011.

Social engineering takes on many faces. Attackers take advantage of human behaviors to obtain access or steal information. As we've seen, social engineers often appear unassuming or respectable authority figures and use fabricated stories and personalities.

The Art of Intrusion: The Real Stories Behind the Exploits of Hackers, Intruders and Decivers, by Kevin Mitnick

The Cuckoo's Egg: Tracking A Spy, by Cliff Stoll

Liars & Outliers, by Bruce Schneier

Chapter 2: Influencing Techniques

The true power of social engineering is manifested when those wielding the knowledge to manipulate people succeed in influencing others into compliance. Many tactics and theories discussed in this book may be considered unethical in certain situations. However, the tactics examined here should be used for ethical purposes only.

This chapter, we'll examine several tactics used by social engineers to influence people through such strategies as: reciprocity, authority, scarcity and others.

The following topics will be covered in this chapter:

- Reciprocity
- Authority
- Scarcity
- Likability
- Concession and Obligation

Social engineering has adapted over the years to include aspects of technology, as demonstrated in the previous chapter. But at its core, technology is merely an instrument leveraged toward getting people to do things they might not otherwise do. The fuel that makes a social engineering attack possible is one's own ability to influence people. That's the true power of social engineering – manipulating people to do your will.

In this section, we are going to examine a few tactics for influencing others. The foundation for the tactics to follow has been borrowed, in part, from the evidence-based research conducted by Robert B. Cialdini. Dr. Cialdini is a leading author in the subject of influence and persuasion. His book, *Influence: The Psychology of Persuasion* is recommended for a thorough study on the art and science of persuasion.

Reciprocity

Reciprocity in social psychology refers to an intrinsic expectation that a positive action should be rewarded with another positive action. In essence, this creates a "something for something" situation. For example, you feel obligated to thank someone who holds the door open for you. When used in the right context, reciprocity can be a very effective and influential, yet easy, social engineering tactic to execute. However reciprocity can render itself ineffective if the attacker acts as if they are owed a favor. Therefore, it is essential for the positive reaction to be given without strings attached and of decent value to the target.

One of the most fruitful ways of utilizing the reciprocity tactic is while trying to obtain physical access to a target location. This can be accomplished by hanging out in the smoker's area and offering to light someone's cigarette. It just may prompt someone to reciprocate the kind gesture by holding the door open for you. It's also a very effective technique when trying to bypass a receptionist or guard desk.

Authority

From a young age, people are taught to respect parents, aunts, uncles, teachers, police and more. It is a principle that is instilled in all of us from early childhood and follows us through adulthood. Leveraging the authority tactic is effective when a social engineer is purporting to be a person of authority that holds power over the target, such as a CTO. Studies show that people are far more apt to follow instructions from a person with a position of authority, legitimate or otherwise. What's more, the use of the authority tactic has even been found be to effective if the person of authority is not physically present.

Social engineers make heavy use of authority tactics by pretending to be executive management, vendors or business partners. The perceived notion of authority is all it takes for a target to forego their best judgment.

Before purporting to be an authority figure, be sure your client gives the okay. Also, please be aware of any legal implications of doing so, such as posing as a law enforcement officer.

Dr. Cialdini's book mentions a few types of authority: legal, organizational and social. The legal type of authority is one typically used by government and law. While purporting to be a police officer during a social engineering test may be highly effective, it is also illegal. Therefore, this kind of activity is not advised and should be avoided at all costs.

As the name implies, organizational authority applies to someone at an organization that maintains some level of power, such as a C-level executive or a manager. Social engineers often leverage this type of authority to persuade less senior staff into compliance. It has been proven to be highly effective if the victim believes the attacker maintains some level of power over them.

Social authority is about perceived social status. The key word here is "perceived." That is to say, individuals tend to react to situation of social authority based upon representations of authority versus material authority. This type of authority can be used to apply peer pressure to a target while playing upon the target's desire to be liked. It also plays on the victims desire to comply with the social authority, or leader, such that obedience will likely benefit the victim in doing so.

Examples of social authority may be projected through one's body language or one's way of speaking, such as name-dropping of high-ranking individuals. Material things such as clothes and cars are also highly regarded social status indicators. Thus, they play a significant part in the establishment of social authority.

Scarcity

In social engineering, scarcity is used to create a situation or feelings of urgency necessitating the target to make a quick and rash decision. Of course, the scarcity situation itself is one that is fabricated by the social engineering and the choices provided are not in the best interest of the target. The desired outcome is one that forces the target to go against their instinct and comply with the social engineer's request.

One highly effective scarcity scheme in a social engineering campaign is to combine it with the authority tactic. For example, an attacker could fabricate a scenario whereby an individual has telephoned the company help desk with an urgent request. He or she is trying to give an important presentation but has been locked out of his or her account. The individual needs the account unlocked and the password changed to "password" immediately. For added benefit, the social engineer could leverage the authority tactic by purporting to be the company's COO whose presentation happens to be for the board of directors.

Combining influencing tactics, such as authority and scarcity, can strengthen any social engineering campaign for maximum results.

Likability

Who doesn't enjoy being liked? For most of us, we enjoy the feeling and tend to subconsciously reciprocate by liking the person back. It's part of human nature, really. As a result, this is a powerful tool that social engineers exploit often. But it should be noted, though, it is not an easy tactic to pull off.

There are a few key items to consider when using this tactic. First of all, positive reinforcement is useful. Simple, yet tactful, compliments are effective. Saying something like, "you're beautiful!" is far too much. Complimenting someone on their voice, shoes, watch or car is effective yet still in the safe zone. When you compliment target during his or her normal day, it may throw him or her off and create an awkward situation. To avoid that, always follow up a compliment with a simple question. This allows the target to accept the compliment, regroup/respond to you while avoiding any awkward silence. For example, "You have a pleasant accent. Where are you from?" Or, "That's a great looking watch. May I ask where you bought it?"

It's important to project a confident, upbeat demeanor. Doing so will positively impact any social engineering attempt. People like confident people and tend to find them socially attractive. Be careful not to project a cocky or arrogant attitude. Speak with an authoritative tone; yet be humble in your speech. Always wear a smile and dress nicely or wear situation-appropriate clothing. It is important to blend in with the surroundings. Speech should match the surroundings as well. For example, business style dialog is probably not appropriate for pool hall environments.

Naturally, the goal is to establish a rapport with the target. This can be accomplished through tactful compliments, a positive demeanor and a confident aura. People tend to like others who share the same thoughts and opinions, but people also like others who happen to look like them. No, it doesn't mean you need to be their twin. What we are really talking about here is surface appearance. The style of dress should be situation appropriate and resemble, but not match, the target. Avoid standing out like a sore thumb. This sends an unwanted message that you're different and instills an automatic sense of distrust or wariness in others.

We want the to get the target to open up via conversation. This is an effective way to break down barriers, especially if the target is in a call center somewhere. You can't necessarily compliment them on their shoes. Depending upon the situation, it could be very difficult to get the target to engage in a conversation.

In my early years working on a help desk, I recall running on autopilot throughout the day. I devoted very little of myself to actual conversation. There is no limit to the number of things you can use to spark a conversation. In these situations, the real challenge is time. With a little creativity, topics as mundane as the weather can spark a conversation with any call center representative running on autopilot. Once they're engaged, "Liking" strategies can begin.

Concession

Earlier in this chapter we discussed reciprocation and how it's used to foster a quid pro quo situation. Concessions are somewhat similar but are a bit more direct and tricky to navigate. The root word of concession is concede. To concede is to acknowledge or make an admission of defeat. It also means to give away something, usually in a reluctant manner.

In the context of social engineering, a concession might involve a social engineer asking a victim for their social security number, expecting some resistance. The social engineer then lowers his expectation (cost) by saying the victim could instead visit a website and enter it him or herself. Because the social engineer conceded by lowering the "cost," the victim feels compelled to oblige and meet halfway.

Concession tactics are a form of bargaining whether the victim knows it or not. Of course, if this is apparent it may not sit well with the victim. They may sense something fishy and clam up. As a result you may lose rapport and a position with which to negotiate.

To a social engineer, losing your credibility is detrimental. You may have only one chance at it and there's no room to make a mistake. As I mentioned earlier, social engineering plans that involve concession strategies must be handled with tact. My advice is to use concession strategies sparingly and only when confidence is high.

Obligation

According to Wikipedia, obligation is defined as a course of action that someone is required to take as a result of a legal or social requirement. In the social engineering context, we generally refer to a situation where an attacker gives a target something of value. In turn, the target feels (socially) obligated to return the favor. It could be a kind gesture, information or a physical item of value to the target.

When using the obligation tactic, it must be carried out with a genuine demeanor. If the target thinks you expect something in return, he or she may resist. It's important for the target to feel as if they are rewarding you by their own free will.

An example of an obligation tactic might be as simple as holding the door open for the target. It may start with a tasteful compliment. Either way, the obligation must be worth something to the target in order for them to reciprocate. Personally, I've found the best techniques begin with a compliment and lead into some level of personal conversation. By personal, I mean some topic the target feels a certain affinity toward. This might be sports, family, music, etc. The list goes on. Discovering what the target has an affinity toward is typically discovered during the information-gathering phase. Information gathering will be discussed in later chapters of this book.

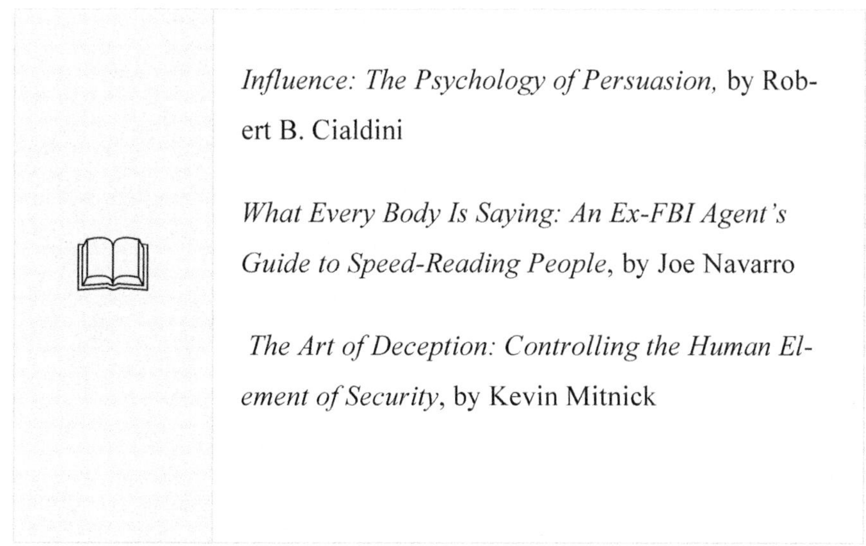

Influence: The Psychology of Persuasion, by Robert B. Cialdini

What Every Body Is Saying: An Ex-FBI Agent's Guide to Speed-Reading People, by Joe Navarro

The Art of Deception: Controlling the Human Element of Security, by Kevin Mitnick

Chapter 3: Elicitation

Government intelligence agencies as well as business intelligence collectors use elicitation tactics. Their only role is to covertly obtain non-public information from their targets. Many of the tactics and theories discussed in this book may be considered unethical in certain situations. For that reason, the tactics examined here should be used for ethical purposes only.

In this chapter, we'll examine several tactics used by social engineers to extract valuable information using strategies like: flattery, bracketing and artificial ignorance. Effective elicitation should be completely transparent to the victim and they may never know they were once a target.

The following topics will be covered in this chapter:

- Flattery
- False statements
- Artificial ignorance
- The sounding board
- Bracketing and more…

According to the definition by the FBI, elicitation is a technique used to discreetly gather information. That is to say, elicitation is the strategic use of casual conversation to extract information from targets without giving them the feeling that they are being interrogated. Elicitation attacks can be simple or involve complex cover stories, planning and even co-conspirators. What is most important is that the elicitation attempt by the social engineer appears genuine to the target. Otherwise, the target may grow suspicious and become non-responsive.

Elicitation may seem stealthy and spy-like, but the truth is many of us have used it multiple times over during our lives. For example, have you ever tried to plan a surprise birthday party and needed to know their schedule without letting them on to your plans? Have you ever tried to ask what your spouse wants for an anniversary gift without tipping them off?

Many intelligence agencies, law enforcement officers and military personnel use elicitation tactics during interviews and interrogations.

There are many techniques to elicit information from a target. Social engineers have found it be useful to combine these techniques with other types of social engineering. The following is a brief list of just a few of those elicitation techniques.

Flattery

The use of flattery goes a long way in sweet-talking a target into giving up additional information. Statements such as, "You seem like a top-notch guy. I'll bet you were the brains behind that project" is sometimes all that is needed to kick start valuable elicitation. Flattery seems like an obvious tactic, but it is proven to be very effective when done skillfully.

Bragging is something that is frowned up in the West. People are often proud of their achievements, but find little opportunity to share them due to the stigma. When we compliment a person, it generally opens the door for bragging. For example, after we compliment a target they will likely feel compelled to elaborate on his or her involvement on a project. Even if he or she is downplaying the compliment, the target is talking about the subject and possibly giving up information. A good social engineer should exploit that opportunity by digging deeper.

An important note to mention is that exaggerated flattery about a target's accomplishments rarely backfires. Because of the stigma attached to bragging, this usually compels the target to normalize their accomplishments to the attacker. This is good because it gets the target to open up. A chatty target can be a gold mine of information to a social engineer.

On the other hand, exaggerated flattery when referring to a target's clothes or persona, for example, can be disastrous. This approach must be handled with tact. Sexual harassment or borderline sexual harassment statements should never be a part of a social engineering plan. Therefore, it should be avoided at all costs. Instead, compliments should be directed away from personal features and appearance and toward more material things. For example, shoes, watches, briefcases, glasses, purses, automobiles, etc.

False Statements

This tactic involves stating a deliberate false statement in the hopes that the target will correct you with the accurate information. A useful statement might be, "I heard they have seventeen cameras, twelve guards and a fingerprint scanners in their lobby. They say that place is like Fort Knox! Nobody can get in."

The key to this tactic is to include details and greatly exaggerate the scenario. For example, if the objective is to learn about the number of cameras in the lobby, be sure to grossly exaggerate the number. Do not simply say that there are several cameras in the lobby. The goal is to get the target to correct you by stating the correct number. If someone is spouting off incorrect information, such as the number of cameras, when all the while we know the undeniable truth, it's part of human nature to want to educate that person. It is that human behavioral characteristic that sits at the core of this tactic and is exactly what we want to tease out.

It's worth mentioning that if the false statements are too close to reality, the target may not feel obligated to correct you. Again, the key is to overstate with detail so that the target feels compelled to correct you with detail.

Artificial Ignorance

As described in the previous section, false and grandiose statements play on human behavior triggering a reaction to correct incorrect statements. Much in the same manner, humans have an intrinsic desire to teach and educate others. Social engineers use artificial ignorance to pretend to be inexperienced on a topic in order to instigate a reaction by the target to educate them. A useful statement might be, "I don't know anything about motion detectors, but I'll bet the cops are here often. I heard they go off all the time due to shadows from the trees." The intrinsic desire to teach is especially notable where the "teacher" has an affinity toward the subject matter or works in the industry. Leveraging subject matter the target has an affinity toward will increase the chances he or she will feel compelled to educate you.

Blending elicitation tactics increases the opportunity for success. From my own personal experience, conjoining flattery tactics with artificial ignorance has been proven to be very effective. The two accompany each other extremely well as elicitation strategies. For example, playing dumb about the function of motion cameras while responding to the target with flattering comments. Boosting egos tends to open people up to conversation much easier. A chatty target is a good target. It also creates a likeness between the social engineer and the target. As we mentioned in an earlier chapter, likeness is a powerful tool for influencing others.

The Sounding Board

The sounding board takes advantage of the human behavior to brag or grumble about their feelings. An immediate kinship is created transparently when a person confides their feelings in another individual, even perfect strangers. He or she will likely give up more information as a result. The key to successfully leveraging the sounding board tactic is to listen intently, patiently and validate his or her feelings.

A well-executed sounding board tactic is one of the most effective elicitation techniques. It is often difficult to get targets to speak at-length. So, to keep the target talking, do not interject too often and allow for moments of silence. Silence is uncomfortable for most people, so they have a tendency to keep talking to avoid awkward silence.

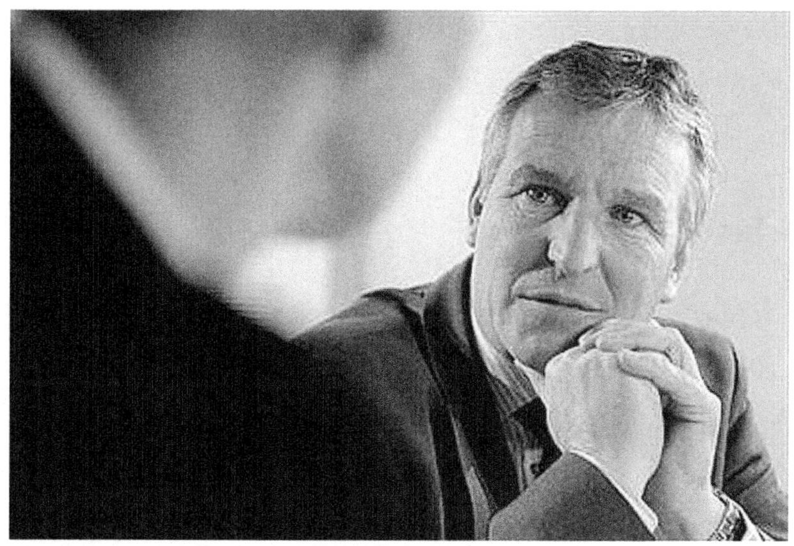

Social engineers frequently play on the instinct to brag or share exploitable information with complete strangers. A good social engineer can create a "safe" environment for the victim to brag or complain. One way to do this is by validating *all* of the target's feelings, positive or negative. This creates a connection between the engineer and the victim. By the social engineer depicting himself as a person they will never ever meet again also creates a safe environment. As a result, it lessens the potential for negative judgment from the stranger and in turn, increases the chances for additional disclosure by the target. In essence, it sends a signal that no negative sharing is off the table and opens up the floodgates.

At the root of the sounding board tactic is being a good listener. This is easier said than done. The social engineer must make frequent eye contact with body language that says, I'm interested in what you're saying. Secondly, agreeing with what the target's thoughts and validating them by sharing some of your own similar experiences or fabricating them.

Bracketing

This technique is used is used by social engineers to elicit more precise information from a target. To accomplish this, a very high or very low approximation is given in an effort to entice the victim to respond with a more specific number. For example, if the goal is to learn about the number of motion detectors in the lobby. The social engineer might say to the target, "I'd guess their security is pretty tight. I would assume they have fifteen motion detectors in their lobby."

From a personal angle, I make heavy use of bracketing tactics specifically when trying to learn about the physical security makeup of a building or room. Most security guards I've encountered rather enjoy opportunities to either complain or brag about the environments they protect. I will say that most of them have a tendency to have pride in the environments they protect. As a result, they like to talk about how secure they are. If the objective is to learn about the number of motion detectors from security guards, be sure to pump their egos a bit. However, intentionally lowball the number of motion detectors. This will likely trigger them to correct you with a glimmer of pride in their eye when they reveal there are actually ten motion detectors! Now that you've pumped up their ego, they are primed for other elicitation techniques.

Confidential Baiting

Confidential baiting involves the development of a conversation where the social engineer pretends to divulge confidential information to the victim. This is done in the hopes that the victim will reciprocate with sensitive information of their own.

An example of confidential baiting might resemble a scenario where the social engineer says to the target, "You didn't hear this from me... but Company XYZ's security cameras don't actually record anything." Confiding sensitive information to another person usually triggers reciprocation. It is sort of a natural occurring quid pro quo situation. Once again, the objective is for the target to reciprocate with sensitive information in return.

When confidential baiting is used, it is important to bait the target with information as close to the kind of information you are seeking from the client.

One important consideration to remember is that the nature of the sensitive information being divulged to the target must be similar to the nature of the information being sought out by the victim. This offers the best chance the target will reciprocate with something about their company's security cameras. Of course, the bait must be of some interest the target for it to have any value. Selecting the right bait will come with a little research.

No matter what the objective, as social engineers we may use any opportunity to elicit information from victims, at conferences, on the street or over the phone. However, the key to an effective elicitation attempt involves a little bit of planning while being able read and respond to the target skillfully.

I'm going to pause for a moment to recommend additional reading material on the topic elicitation. An author by the name of Frank Stopa wrote a book titled, *The Human Skills: Elicitation and Interviewing*. The book does a great job covering elicitation strategies and I highly recommend some of the tactics described. According to the book's introduction, the techniques have been used to extract valid admissions from hardened criminals and individuals in the business world as well.

The author is a former intelligence officer with years of elicitation experience, domestic and abroad. I should also mention that the book seems to target the law enforcement industry. This is especially noted in the interviewing area of the book. However, many of the principles described can be applied toward the business world and social engineering.

It's Not All About Me: The Top Ten Techniques for Building Quick Rapport with Anyone, by Robin Dreeke

Find Out Anything From Anyone, Anytime: Secrets of Calculated Questioning From a Veteran Interrogator, by James Pyle

The Human Skills: Elicitation and Interviewing, by Frank Stopa

Chapter 4: Pretexting

Due to its creative element and limitless opportunities, pretexting is one of the most fascinating forms of social engineering. Many of the tactics and theories discussed in this book may be considered unethical in certain situations. For that reason, the tactics examined here should be used for ethical purposes only.

In this chapter, we'll examine several tactics used by social engineers to manipulate targets through the fabrication of invented scenarios known as pretexts. We'll cover some of the most common pretexting tactics and learn through research and planning exercises.

The following topics will be covered in this chapter:

- Research and planning
- Legal considerations
- Body language
- Expression

As previously mentioned, social engineering is an exploitation of trust between the social engineer and the target. During live social engineering attacks, there usually isn't much time to build trust. Part of the process to establish trust quickly is done by leveraging pretexting techniques.

Pretexting involves fabricating invented scenarios and stories in order to persuade a target to divulge information or do something. It may sound like that's what we've been discussing all along in this chapter. But pretexting, within the context of social engineering, goes far beyond flattery or pretending to be ignorant on a subject. Instead, it may involve elaborate planning, identity impersonation and even disguises. Generally speaking, all of this work is designed to quickly establish trust with the target in the hopes he or she will comply. A social engineering attack is doomed without a well-planned pretext that establishes trust with the target.

Pretexting is used by different industries with different goals in mind. Skip Tracers use pretexts to create fabricated scenarios in an attempt to locate the whereabouts of individuals. Law enforcement officers use pretexts during interrogations while trying to get suspects to confess or divulge certain information.

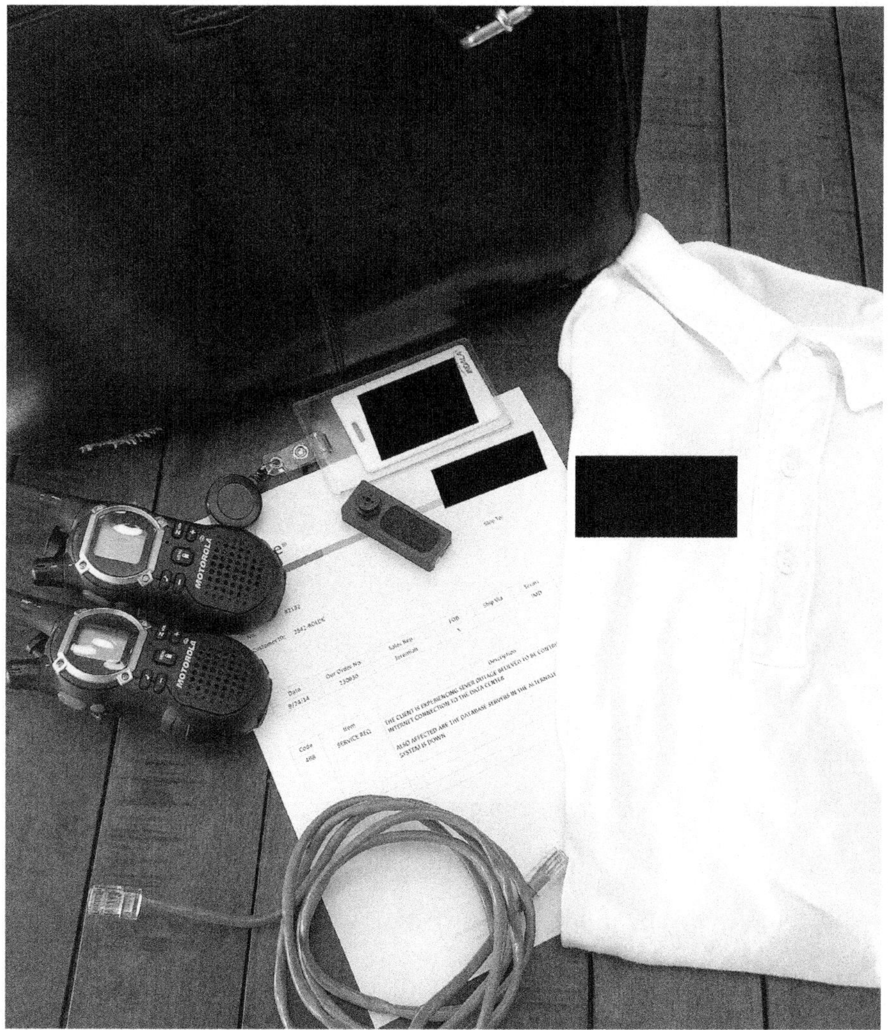

Pretexting equipment: radio, fake badge, fake work order, work shirt, pinhole camera and IT tool bag

Pretexts don't have to be complex to be successful. One example might involve a social engineer purporting to be a copier repairperson who needs physical access into the mailroom. What is ultimately going to convince the target that he or she is there on official business comes down to three primary goals: acting the part, looking the part and believing they are the part. The latter goal is what requires the most practice.

What is also important to know about pretexting is that there are no one-size fits all scenarios. As the saying goes, "There is more than one way to skin a cat." Social engineers may leverage a handful of pretexts with which they are comfortable. However, it is imperative he/she not become too comfortable with carrying out only a few pre-texts. That kind of behavior stints development and is counterproductive to successful pretexting.

The foundation for all successful social engineering attempts is re-search. By research, I don't mean just researching the target. That is of great importance, no doubt. I mean that a social engineer must con-tinually invent new and innovative pretexts to stay ahead of the targets. Some security-savvy organizations train their users about so-cial engineering topics frequently and consistently. Thus, it is crucial to push the envelope in terms of creativity and innovation.

The following is a list of pretexting ideologies that you can leverage during testing. This is definitely not an exhaustive list, but it's enough to communicate the spirit of what pretexting is about.

Research & Planning

Research should be the longest and most involved leg of the social engineering planning process. If it isn't, you're probably doing something wrong. Nowhere else is there a more direct correlation between success and the amount of research performed when preparing for a social engineering attempt. This point simply cannot be underscored enough.

So far we've established that pretexting can be very powerful and a relatively quick way to obtain valuable information from a target. But before we can start off and begin researching, we must first consider the following:

- What is/are the objective(s)?
- What information am I after?
- What issues and questions am I trying to raise?
- What do I already know about my target(s)?
- What are the rules of engagement (RoE)?

When performing a social engineering test for clients, the aforementioned bullet points must be addressed and answered for each assessment. There could be more, but this list represents a decent foundation from which to expand upon.

First and foremost, a social engineering attempt's objective must be clearly stated in a few clearly defined, short sentences.

A sample objective might look like the following example:

> **Objective:** to assess the staff's adherence to the visitor policy and efficacy of routine rogue device/bug sweeps.

Once the objective has been defined and agreed upon, it's important to briefly state the general approach in which the objective will be carried out. This could change during the course of the actual test and social engineers must be prepared for it. However, the "plan A" methodology must be documented from a high level.

In order to identify the approach, some basic information gathering is necessary. Information gathering itself, depending upon the objective, can amount to be a fairly complex process. Consequently, information gathering will be covered in a later chapter. For the purposes of the planning phase exercise, let's assume that preliminary work has been completed and that we have a high level approach planned.

A sample approach might look like the following example:

> **Approach:** access he executive boardroom via covert/overt means and plant both an audio listening device and a PlugBot network listening device.

Once the objective and approach have been identified the next step should involve what kind of information that is to be gathered. Using our example, the data we might want to gather would include audio captures of confidential board meetings. Another dataset we might want to capture is any network traffic acquired by the PlugBot device.

So far we've identified our objective, planned an approach and identified the type of data that we're after. High level planning of this kind keeps the mission at-hand focused and efficient from the start. Latter phases of the social engineering process will benefit from this kind of work done early on. Progressing further in the planning phase, we are ready to begin the drafting process for a test plan.

A tactical outline for accomplishing the objective is the next logical step in the planning process. Not only is the test plan a project work paper, but also more importantly it serves as an outline of the steps to be carried out by the social engineer(s). If conducting this assessment for a client, it is important to note that the action steps in the test plan must be commensurate with the estimated level of threat against the organization. In other words, the test plan should include the actions that an actual attacker might take in terms of complexity, cost, tools and approach.

A sample test plan might look like the following example:

TEST PLAN - TAP THE DATA CENTER

- Arrive at location during lunch
- Park vehicle hidden from lobby and other windows
- Enter the premises through the front lobby
- Engage the lobby receptionist, flash work order and request IT dept. staffer for access to data center for maintenance issue
- Establish maintenance issue pretext with IT staffer and persuade him/her to grant access to data center
    - Use pre-recorded phone call "last resort" to embellish urgency if IT staffer isn't cooperating
- Obtain access to data center
- Visually scan the data center for the target computer and an ideal location for the PlugBot
- Remove electronics equipment from bag and stall for no longer than ten minutes
    - If still escorted, ask escort to borrow a piece of equipment likely not located in the vicinity
- Install keylogger on target system
- Remove PlugBot from bag and install it
- Indicate the issue has been contained
- Exit

Equipment list: driver's license, utility uniform, utility tool bag, hardware keylogger, PlugBot, Ethernet cable, radio, phony ID badge, clipboard, phony work order, radio and cell phone with *pre-recorded audio

By now it should be evident what sort of questions we aim to address as a result of the test. Borrowing from the sample objective earlier in this chapter, the questions we aim to address might look like the following example:

1) How well does staff observe their company's visitor policy?
2) Does staff challenge unknown/unescorted visitors?
3) How effective is the company's security awareness program?
4) How easy is it to covertly infiltrate the premises?
5) How effective is the organization's rogue device-sweeping program?
6) How trivial was it to capture audio from the boardroom?

At the end of the social engineering test, these and other questions may be answered. Ultimately, they will provide the client with valuable information about the measured vulnerabilities within their organization.

Legal Considerations

Some areas of information security tend to fall into grey areas. For example, some technologists may argue that software bug hunting and the concept of full disclosure lies within the fringes of ethical behavior. I've even spoken with some application developers who consider application penetration testing to be disrespectful and unethical. Whatever your stance on the debate, when it comes to social engineering, one thing is true. Without rules of engagement and an agreed-upon approach, social engineering certainly has potential to step on the big toe of ethical hacking. For example, pretending to be a police officer or damaging property. Therefore, it is absolutely imperative that social engineers establish boundaries with clients and stay well within the law.

The Rules of Engagement (RoE) is an agreed upon plan with the social engineering team and the client for carrying out a social engineering test. The RoE must accompany each and every social engineering test. It must be followed strictly by all team members.

When performing social engineering work for a client, the Rules of Engagement (RoE) plan describes how the test will be carried out. More importantly, it specifically calls out tactics and actions that are out-of-scope for social engineers. For example, the RoE might state that tactics resulting in damage to company property are out of bounds behavior. It may state that spear phishing is out of scope. Or, it might call out something as simple as the time of day for testing. A RoE is an agreed-upon plan between the tester and the target involving what tactics are allowed and which ones aren't. In any situation, a RoE is a good idea and should be mandatory for every consulting engagement.

Body Language

First and foremost, body language and expression are immense and complex topics that are too large to cover in this book. For that reason, I am forced to only scratch the surface on the subject. But I will make every attempt to touch on the most foundational elements. For a thorough study on the subject, I personally recommend the following publications:

- *What Every Body Is Saying* by Joe Navarro
- *Introducing NLP: Psychological Skill for Understanding and Influencing People* by Joseph O'Connor
- *The Definitive Book of Body Language* by Allan and Barbara Pease

Positioning

Quite a bit can be said with non-verbal communication. That's precisely why body language and gesturing is so deep-rooted in personal communication. And the link to social engineering is no different. When used properly, gestures can direct your target's thought process subconsciously. So it's important for social engineers to understand the basic elements of body language.

Hands, feet, arms and torso all are very telling about a person in their own way. So it's important to be cognizant of these visual cues when reading a target. As social engineers, we will also want to send visual signals to our targets as well. Our social engineering plan may call for us to be authoritative. Therefore, we may stand up straight and assume an air of confidence about us, without being too threatening. If in a seated position, we may choose to steeple our hands, without looking too stiff.

Police interrogators make some of the best body language experts. They are able to pick up on the most subtle body positioning cues and mannerisms. It is often said that, "the lips lie but the body tells the truth."

People talk with their hands, albeit, some more than others. I'm guilty of it and it seems even more exaggerated when I'm nervous. When engaging a target for the first time, it's natural to get a little nervous. People who are nervous tend to fidget with their hands or an object, like a pen or piece of paper. As a matter of fact, I always get a shot of nervousness when engaging a target. But as social engineers, we must never show it. With time and practice, the nervousness subsides.

So what can we do to suppress nervousness? Aside from rehearsing? Not much. What we really should be doing is focusing on how to hide our nervousness.

Here are a few tips on body placement to help hide nervousness:

- Hands should be free of any objects to prevent fidgeting (especially click pens)
- Avoid the temptation to touch your hair as this is a sign of insecurity
- Keep your arms and hands at your side – avoid the temptation to cross your arms or hold them up and against your belly area as this is a sign of nervousness/uncertainty
- Avoid touching your ears, especially when leveraging authoritative tactics, as this is a sign of indecisiveness
- This one goes without saying – refrain from finger drumming
- If standing, avoid the temptation to sway or tap your foot
- Know thyself – take an inventory of what nervous ticks you have and practice hiding them

Emulating

One of my favorite gestures is called emulating. Essentially, it boils down to copying the gestures and body positioning of the target. You may wonder why this is even a thing. Honestly, it is an efficient way to establish a non-verbal rapport with your target. In my early days, I often made use of emulating during job interviews. When you emulate the target, you create a subconscious sense of connection with that person. Consequently, you appear more likeable in his or her eyes. Obviously, this puts you in a better position of power and persuasion.

Now, it's worth mentioning that the target's each and every move should not be emulated. He or she would catch on eventually and it would likely turn into a rather awkward situation. People use subtle gestures all the time without really knowing it. So the objective is to mimic those subtle gestures.

Here are a few tips for emulating:

- Select at least two repeated gestures and emulate them sparingly (e.g.: raising pen to mouth, etc.)
- Match the volume of your voice to the target's volume
- Emulate the target's body position (e.g.: leaning back in chair, standing, crossed legs, etc.)

- Match the speed at which the target speaks to your own
- Square up your body position to the target's position
- Lastly, do not overdo it!

Anchoring

The concept of anchoring has its origins in the study of Neuro-Linguistic Programming (NLP). NLP is an approach to communication by linking neurological processes, language and behavioral patterns through "programming." What does that mean? Well, the concept of NLP is that it can be used in casual conversation to subliminally condition the mind, yours or others. As an aside, the concept is somewhat controversial in terms of validity. Some people think it's pure hogwash. Some people consider it evil mind control while others claim that it's useful for personal enrichment purposes. Personally I believe it works, but I'm a firm moderate on the subject. I've seen its effects firsthand, but I personally don't believe all the hype. But I digress.

Anchoring is essentially all about association of statements while using some sort of physical gesture to do so. That is to say, language is used to associate two or more statements and gestures are the medium to link them together. The underlying objective is persuasive in nature. In other words, the purpose of anchoring is to subconsciously persuade the target toward one way of thinking.

Though the concept of anchoring might sound somewhat cryptic, it is actually used fairly significantly outside of social engineering. In fact, some sales people use anchoring as a sales tactic. For example, let's assume a situation where a target and a sales person are sitting across from one another at table. During casual conversation, the sales person may make a reference about how bad the traffic is in the city. This will generally generate some kind of agreeable response by the target. A head nod or otherwise. After all, bad traffic is something that all of us can relate to. This is step one in the anchoring setup. While describing the bad traffic, he puts his left hand on the table forming a roadblock hand gesture. The negative association has now been built. Now it needs to be reinforced two or more time during the course of the conversation and with similar associations.

For a more thorough study on the science of Neuro-Linguistic Programming (NLP), please see the following book titled: *Introducing NLP: Psychological Skills for Understanding and Influencing People (Neuro-Linguistic Programming),* by Joseph O'Connor.

Link:
http://books.google.com/books/about/Introducing_NLP.html?id=rwoiMLdu9eIC

Moving forward in the conversation, the sales person will now go on to describe and build positive thoughts. For example, a funny story about his daughter or a fun trip to the cabin. During these stories, the sales person uses his right hand to gesture and punctuate the best highlights of the story. My favorite gesture is a form of the famous "Bill Clinton thumb smash." If you're not familiar, imagine you are holding an invisible remote control. Since the thumb smash is an often joked about gesture, you'll want to augment your thumb smash a bit.

At this point, the sales person has, in so many words, conditioned the target's thinking. The left hand roadblock hand gesture is associated with something bad. The right hand thumb smash means something is good. By now in the conversation, the sales person will attempt to convince the target to purchase services from his company instead of the competing company. The sales person begins with describing the services by the competitor. But instead of outright bashing the competition, which is what the target expects, something else happens. Instead, the sales person exploits the pre-established anchors to convince the target that his company is better without verbally saying it. In fact, the target already agreed the sales person's company was better once the anchors were established earlier in the conversation. It was simply the sales person's job to make him subconsciously realize it.

Introducing NLP: Psychological Skills for Understanding and Influencing People (Neuro-Linguistic Programming), by Joseph O'Connor

Social Engineering: The Art of Human Hacking, by Christopher Hadnagy

Chapter 5: Information Gathering

In social engineering, information is worth its weight in gold. Even the most seemingly insignificant details can be worth something. Many of the tactics and theories discussed in this book may be considered unethical in certain situations. For that reason, the tactics examined here should be used for ethical purposes only.

Successful social engineering would not be possible without a strong source of information. Information fuels the social engineering plan and is one of the most vital components. In this chapter, we will cover information gathering techniques, sources and tools.

The following topics will be covered in this chapter:

- Overview of Information Gathering
- Information Gathering Techniques
- Sources of Information
- Information Gathering Tools

Overview

Throughout this book we've covered everything from anchoring, flattery, bracketing and baiting to emulating. You might be thinking, how do we support these tactics? How do I know which anchor statements to use? What information do I have at my disposal to use as bait for my target? All of these are important questions that must be answered.

You might be a superstar at confidential baiting. But your efforts, however well thought out they might be, are only as good as the information you have at your fingertips. Not enough research on a target or plan equates to a social engineering attempt that is destined to fail. There are so many social engineering tactics rely heavily on valuable information. Thus, valuable information, for whatever your tactic, must be derived from effective and efficient information gathering practices.

In this chapter, we will start out by discussing techniques used to gather information. Then we will take a look at what sources can be leveraged to collect this information. Finally, I'll briefly introduce a few tools used to carry out information gathering sessions as well as talk about other commonly used social engineering tools.

Before we dig into the specifics of information gathering, we need to talk about how we are going to store this information from the get go. Every social engineering plan involves a multitude of data sources for information. Some information may be derived from eyes-on observation while other information may be obtained from online sources. In either event, we need a central repository to house this data for quick and easy retrieval.

Information Organization

Overview

During a social engineering test, there are likely going to be several things that need to be documented and stored for later use. One of the most prominent is information about targets. What's also important to note is that data sources for targets often arrives from many sources. For example, this could include information gathered from LinkedIn, Facebook, Twitter, forums, Google and others. Managing information from disparate sources can be a challenge. Especially when a team of testers is involved and data must be available to all. Organizing information is essential and it doesn't have to be an overly complex process.

Dradis Framework

Fortunately for us, there are tools freely available designed to help with the task of sharing data across teams. Dradis to the rescue. Dradis is a self-contained web application that provides a consolidated warehouse of information. It is an open source software project that can be found at http://dradisframework.org/.

The Dradis framework is freely available and runs on Linux, Windows, MacOS and FreeBSD systems. Dradis describes itself as tool designed especially for security assessments. As a result, it has plugins for popular security tools, such as: Retina, Zed, Nessus, Nikto and Nmap.

Dradis has a very intuitive collapsible tree menu system. Information is organized into multilevel containers called branches. Notes are entered "free form" and can be categorized for efficient retrieval.

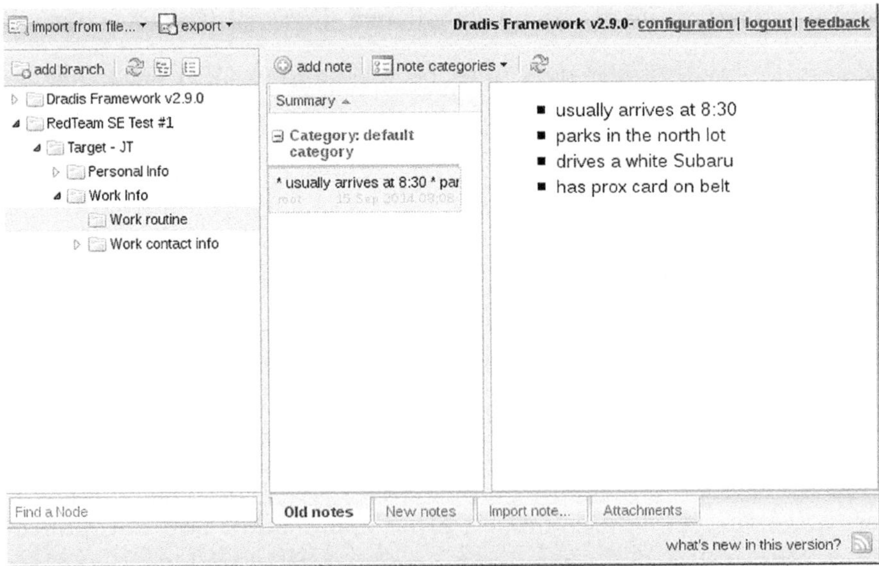

Screenshot of the Dradis Framework v2.9.0

The interface itself is relatively straightforward. The main idea is to provide a mechanism for which to capture information from disparate data sources and that's exactly what Dradis does. From a team perspective, the information in Dradis is viewable and modifiable by all members.

KeepNote

There are other tools to choose from. For example, KeepNote is an alternative to Dradis that is also freely available. KeepNote is quite similar in nature to Dradis, minus the team aspect. It isn't a web application like Dradis, which is the reason behind its single user approach. Under the covers, KeepNote utilizes the same collapsible tree menu as Dradis. From a personal perspective, I like the KeepNote interface better. To me, it just has a better feel to it. For one-person social engineering engagements, KeepNote is perfect for those situations. It can be downloaded at http://keepnote.org/

KeepNote is freely available and capable of running on Linux, Windows (XP, Vista) and Mac OS X platforms. For Linux and Mac OS X, additional third-party libraries are required. Although KeepNote doesn't call itself a security assessment tool, it does come pre-installed on the Kali Linux penetration testing distribution.

KeepNote's user interface allows for quicker and easier rich-text formatting of text. I especially like the ability to add file attachments, screenshots and its full-text search features. All in all, I believe its interface is a little easier to use.

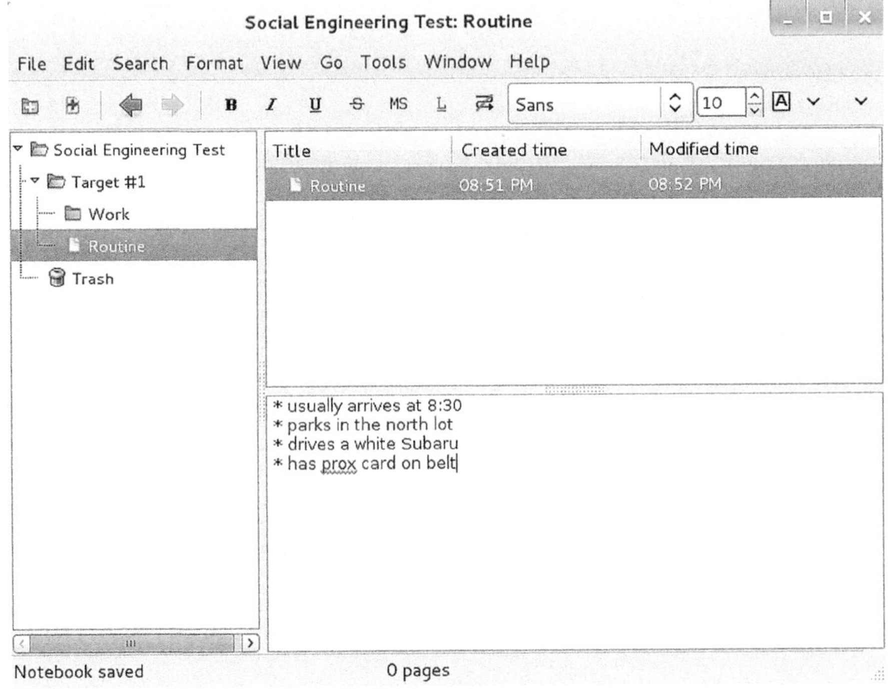

Screenshot of KeepNote 0.7.8

My personal preference, however, leans toward Dradis specifically for team interaction and excellent search capabilities. Either tool will easily accomplish the goal of organizing data efficiently. For the most part, it comes down to personal preference. Whatever the tool you ultimately decide to organize your information, be sure it's one that you feel comfortable working within.

Sources of Information

As any social engineer would tell you, there are many different sources for information gathering. It would not be possible to list each an every source here. But I'll cover the most commonly used sources.

Listed below are the information sources we will cover in this upcoming section:

- Online
- Surveillance
- Trash

Online

Online sources of information are vast and plentiful. Simply imagine what Google and Facebook alone have done to transform the state of online privacy to what it is today. In a matter of a few years short of a decade, these websites have managed to completely change the privacy landscape by making the activities of businesses and people public. What's more, the transformation of the standards for company websites has evolved greatly. Today companies are much more transparent about their inner workings, culture, people and even their political standing. As a result, an organization's website makes another great resource for mining for useful information during a social engineering test.

Naturally, a noteworthy change like these has created an atmosphere where a social engineer is able to obtain information, of a sensitive nature, from not one, but a multitude of online sources quite easily. For that reason alone, many social engineers often rely heavily on online data sources for mining information about a target. And so should you.

Company Website

Mining the company's website for information should be one of the first steps in the information gathering phase. Having said that, not all company websites are created equal. That is to say, not all organizations are as transparent and forthcoming with information as others. However, this should not be a deterrent. There are several ways of finding useful information within a company website, if you know where to look. Hence, a good social engineer should spend a decent amount of time in an attempt to mine that information.

Here are some of the pages/sections of an organization's website that commonly present useful social engineering information:

- Job openings and tech stack information (e.g. Windows, Ubuntu, .NET, PHP, Cisco, firewall technology, Amazon AWS, Rackspace, MS Exchange, etc.)
- The *About* page and mission statements

- Page(s) about the services or products the company provides
- Company leadership and management names and bios
- Any email addresses published on the site
- Naming conventions for email addresses
- Office locations
- Extranets, portals or support sites
- External links (LinkedIn, Facebook, Twitter)

Make good use of Dradis or KeepNote to document any findings as a result of scouring the organization's website. There really is no detail too small or insignificant to document. It may find itself to be very useful in the end.

Search Engines

Google, Bing, Yahoo, DuckDuckGo, Dogpile. There are so many search engines available to use. You may be wondering which would produce fruitful results without having to spend gobs of time re-searching. Each and every search engine has its pros and cons. At the time of this writing, I recommend using Google and Shodan for social engineering purposes. These two engines are an excellent place to start. But by all means, do not limit yourself to my recommendations alone. There is constant progress and innovation in this field.

Google (aka Google Hacking)

First of all, Google indexes everything! Nowadays that is more common knowledge than it was 10 years ago. But, I digress. Google hacking has been around for quite some time. Back in 2005, a security expert by the name of Johnny Long wrote a great book titled, *Google Hacking for Penetration Testers*. It was 448 pages of pure hacker bliss and Johnny set the stage for Google hacking for years to come.

Google hacking does not mean hacking Google itself. It amounts to using advanced Google search operators, called "Google dorks," to tease out a near limitless set of fruitful information. To be more specific, fruitful information that is probably sensitive and not deliberately meant to be publicly available. The dataset includes all sorts of fruitful information, including but not limited to: usernames, passwords, financial information, personal information, credit card numbers and so on. How did it get there? Well, certain ill-informed people put it there unaware that it might be indexed for the entire world to see. And it continues to happen all the time, everyday.

There are entire books dedicated to the study of Google Dorks. The content is far too rich and expansive to be adequately covered here. However, to maximize efforts and not waste time, making heavy use of Google Dorks to find information about the target must be carried out. Thankfully, there is a shortcut. The fine folks at Exploit-DB have taken Johnny Long's work, and the work of others, and made it available online.

This is by no means an exhaustive list, but this shows the standard dorks I initiate as a part of every social engineering test.

- PDF files with text "confidential" inside
  `"<target name here> confidential" filetype:pdf`
- Text with "password" for the target domain
  `ext:sql intext:@<target domain>.com intext:password`
- Word files linked to the target's domain name
  `site:<target domain>.com filetype:doc`
- Visio files linked to the target's domain name
  `site:<target domain>.com filetype:vsd`
- Find network information
  `("DMZ" | "Public IP" | "Private IP") filetype:xls`

The Google Hacking Database can be found online at the following address: http://www.exploit-db/google-dorks/.

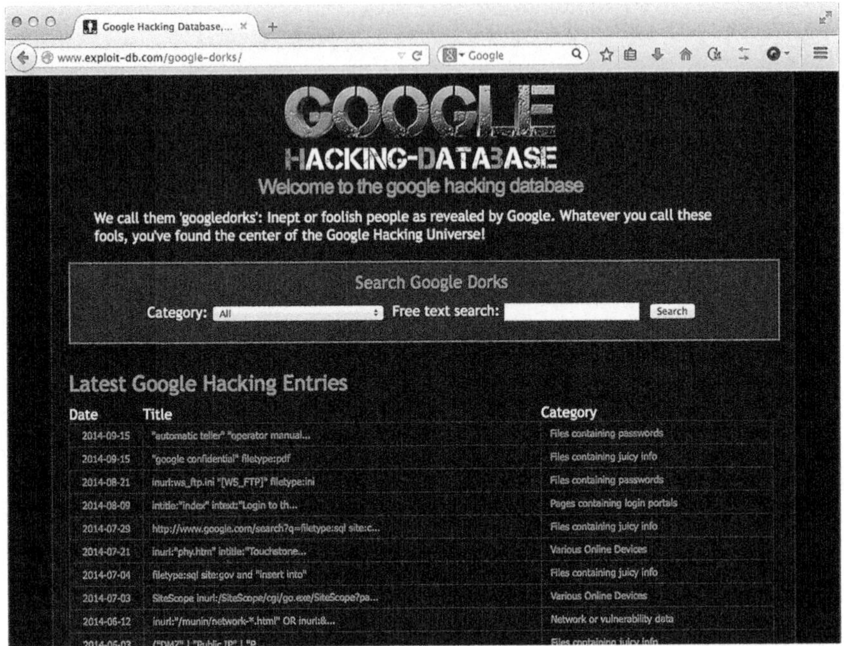

Screenshot of the Google Hacking Database by Exploit-DB.

The best approach toward using Google Dorks, especially if you're a beginner, is to first become familiar with the nomenclature. After a few minutes, the syntax will become clearer. There is a great online resource for making advanced Google searching easier to comprehend. GoogleGuide's advanced operators reference page is a great start.

The Google guide page can be found by navigating here:

http://www.googleguide.com/advanced_operators_reference.html

GoogleGuide.com is designed to be an online interactive tutorial for Google's search capabilities and features. Although it is not an advertised Google Hacking website, it is your one-stop shop reference for learning more about leveraging Google's powerful search parameters.

Shodan Search Engine

According to Wikipedia, Shodan is a search engine that lets you find specific types of computers (routers, servers, etc.) on the Internet using a variety of filters. Some have also described it as a search engine of service banners that are metadata the server sends back to the client when a connection to it is initiated. Essentially, Shodan collects data including, but not limited to: HTTP, FTP, SSH, SNMP, Telnet, MySQL, VNC, etc. The information Shodan indexes consists primarily of information that could be leveraged to exploit those systems. For example, a search for "default password" would yield a number of results for hosts/systems using the default password to gain access to them. The systems vary greatly and include security camera systems, traffic lights, home automation, power plants and more.

Since Shodan's inception in 2009, it has raised some eyebrows in the security industry as well as within mainstream news outlets. CNN

Money called it the scariest search engine on the Internet (http://money.cnn.com/2013/04/08/technology/security/shodan/). Penetration testers abound make heavy use of it, as I'm sure malicious actors do as well.

Screenshot of the Shodan search engine.

Shodan has some very practical uses, especially for penetration testers. But of course, it does lend itself well toward social engineering. This can manifest itself by using Shodan's advanced operators and filters to hone in on target based off specific information.

See here: http://www.shodanhq.com/help/filters

Refine your Shodan search with advanced filters: `geo`, `city`, `country`, `hostname` and `net`. See: http://www.shodanhq.com/help/filters

Shodan will, no doubt, be a great resource for information gathering purposes during a social engineering test. One key aspect to remember is that Shodan is more like casting a wide net for information. In social engineering, we need to be more specific. Thus, in order to gain value from it, you must first normalize and hone in on your target through advanced filters. Information you obtain through refined searches will ultimately be what you're looking for. Some Google dorks are not all that different either. They tend to be broad in nature and without focus toward a specific target. Once again, it is important to refine search parameters so that they're directed toward a specific target in order to gain valuable information.

A decent portion of the information indexed by Shodan is great information for penetration testers as well. Whatever the objectives are, my advice is to ensure the plan and action complies with the Rules of Engagement without stepping out of bounds and into something that resembles a penetration test. Having said that, Shodan will not disappoint as a great resource for information gathering.

Shodan's help page is a great place to become acquainted with it. See: http://www.shodanhq.com/help Be advised, at the time of this writing, Shodan is in the process of updating their page.

WHOIS

The WHOIS database is a free online resource that provides details about domain names. It's actually a query and response protocol used to search the data warehouse containing registered users/assignees of a domain name, IP address block or autonomous system. A WHOIS query can be initiated from the command line in a number of different operating systems. There are websites devoted to performing WHOIS queries as well. See here: http://www.whois.net/

Information contained in WHOIS queries can be very helpful during the initial stages of information gathering. This is especially useful in determining the target's technical contact, email naming convention, physical location and DNS name servers. The information gathered from WHOIS queries can be used to launch a more targeted information gathering expedition.

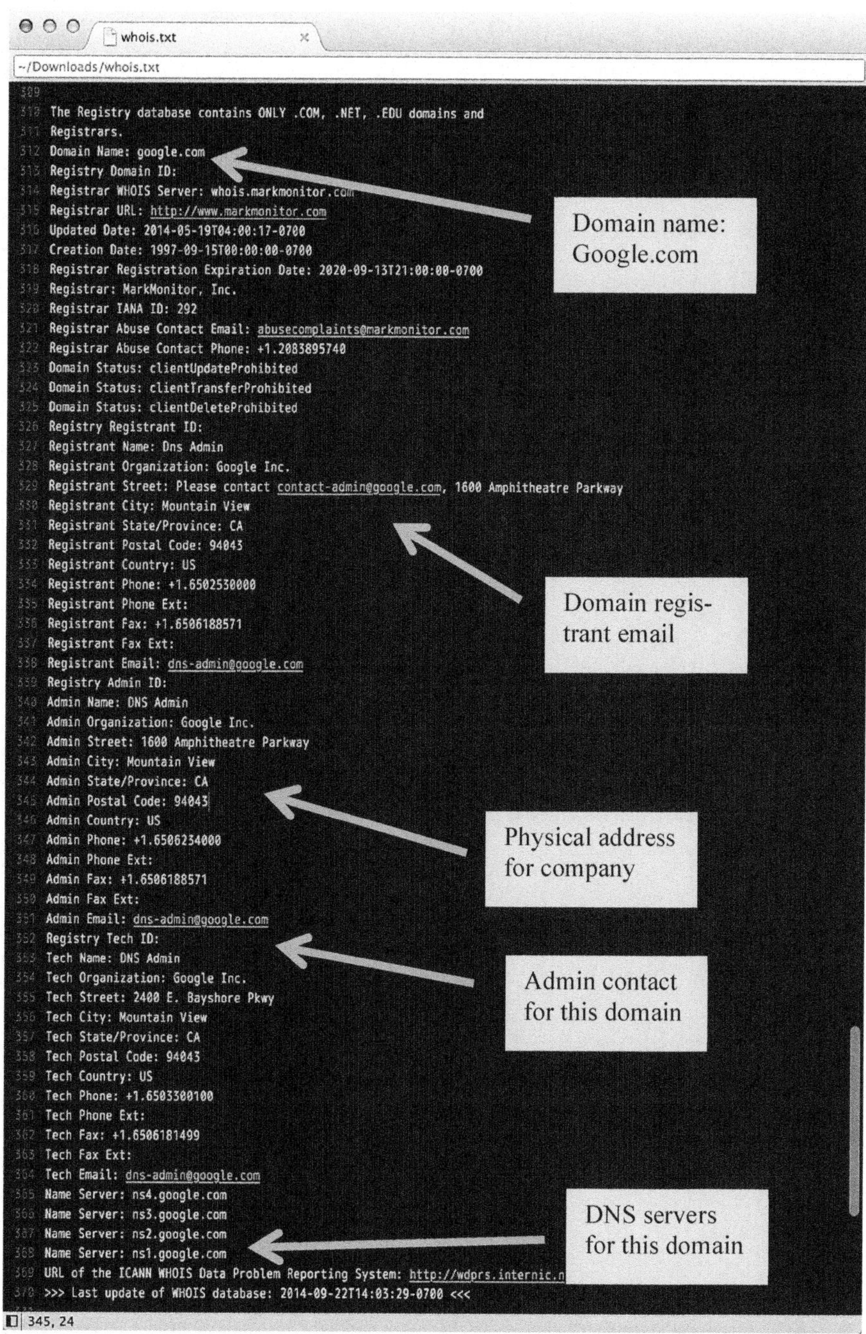
whois.txt

~/Downloads/whois.txt

```
The Registry database contains ONLY .COM, .NET, .EDU domains and
Registrars.
Domain Name: google.com
Registry Domain ID:
Registrar WHOIS Server: whois.markmonitor.com
Registrar URL: http://www.markmonitor.com
Updated Date: 2014-05-19T04:00:17-0700
Creation Date: 1997-09-15T00:00:00-0700
Registrar Registration Expiration Date: 2020-09-13T21:00:00-0700
Registrar: MarkMonitor, Inc.
Registrar IANA ID: 292
Registrar Abuse Contact Email: abusecomplaints@markmonitor.com
Registrar Abuse Contact Phone: +1.2083895740
Domain Status: clientUpdateProhibited
Domain Status: clientTransferProhibited
Domain Status: clientDeleteProhibited
Registry Registrant ID:
Registrant Name: Dns Admin
Registrant Organization: Google Inc.
Registrant Street: Please contact contact-admin@google.com, 1600 Amphitheatre Parkway
Registrant City: Mountain View
Registrant State/Province: CA
Registrant Postal Code: 94043
Registrant Country: US
Registrant Phone: +1.6502530000
Registrant Phone Ext:
Registrant Fax: +1.6506188571
Registrant Fax Ext:
Registrant Email: dns-admin@google.com
Registry Admin ID:
Admin Name: DNS Admin
Admin Organization: Google Inc.
Admin Street: 1600 Amphitheatre Parkway
Admin City: Mountain View
Admin State/Province: CA
Admin Postal Code: 94043
Admin Country: US
Admin Phone: +1.6506234000
Admin Phone Ext:
Admin Fax: +1.6506188571
Admin Fax Ext:
Admin Email: dns-admin@google.com
Registry Tech ID:
Tech Name: DNS Admin
Tech Organization: Google Inc.
Tech Street: 2400 E. Bayshore Pkwy
Tech City: Mountain View
Tech State/Province: CA
Tech Postal Code: 94043
Tech Country: US
Tech Phone: +1.6503300100
Tech Phone Ext:
Tech Fax: +1.6506181499
Tech Fax Ext:
Tech Email: dns-admin@google.com
Name Server: ns4.google.com
Name Server: ns3.google.com
Name Server: ns2.google.com
Name Server: ns1.google.com
URL of the ICANN WHOIS Data Problem Reporting System: http://wdprs.internic.n
>>> Last update of WHOIS database: 2014-09-22T14:03:29-0700 <<<
```

345, 24

Screenshot of WHOIS query of GOOGLE.COM

Social Media, Job Boards & Blogs

A cultural shift has occurred in the last three to five years for many companies. That shift was toward corporate transparency and the adoption of social media as a widely used marketing tool. As I stated earlier in this book, companies use social networks to develop an affinity toward the masses. Nowhere else in history has there been a more direct line of communication between consumer and conglomerate. Companies use Twitter, Facebook, LinkedIn and YouTube to spread their brand in a much more personal way than ever done before. By opening their windows to the world, social engineers have an opportunity to gain better insight into a target with little effort.

Job boards, blogs, wikis and videos also contribute toward creating a closer connection with consumers. Often times, a company website will have the personal email address, Twitter link and LinkedIn account of many of its team members published. Online job postings tend to divulge lots of information about the company's technology stack and sometimes hiring manager information. Social media connections are ideal for social engineers since they tend to be user-centric versus company-centric. There is greater chance of finding out likes, dislikes, schedules and other personal information about targets.

Mining social media for valuable information is and can be very time intensive. Thus, I won't get into the specifics of exploring them individually. Thankfully there is a tool called Maltego that makes the information gathering process far more efficient. We will discuss Maltego in greater detail in the next chapter.

Public Sources

Public sources for collecting information on targets can be acquired through a number of public providers. Public data providers include Intelius, PeopleFinders and US Search. These data providers perform background checks and deliver reports about their subjects for nominal one-time fees or via subscriptions. Although most of the information they provide can be found using search engines, using their services may cut down on manual hours spent trying to dig up the information alone.

- Intelius – http://www.intelius.com
- US Search – http://www.ussearch.com
- PeopleFinders – http://www.peoplefinders.com

Surveillance

Online resources are widely used to gather information for social engineering. In fact, sometimes too much reliance is placed on online information gathering alone. It is important to use a varied approach toward gathering information and not rely on a single data source. Much can be learned about a target through physical surveillance. Of course, if the scope of the test and distance is too great this may not be possible. However, physical surveillance should be mandatory for each and every social engineering test, provided physical distance to the target site is not somehow a hindrance.

Photographic Intelligence

Ideally, a social engineering test should involve as many elements of physical information gathering as possible. The purpose of this is to gather as much intelligence from non-overlapping sources. For example, online information gathering will have some overlapping data between sources. It is best to have a varied background of information versus relying on a single approach.

Photographic intelligence gathering is one effective way of capturing valuable information not likely to be found online. There are many ways of actually acquiring photographic evidence, but here are some of the photos you should obtain from the target:

- **Target Location(s)** – Take as many photos from different angles as possible. This is used to obtain a mental picture of the building, its exits/entrances, approximate size, etc.

- **Point of Entry/Exit** – You should know where every entry point and exit point is located. Take special note of smoking areas, seating areas and other public areas situated near the building. Photograph any security controls used to protect points of entry/exit (cameras, turnstiles).

- **Location of Dumpsters** – Know where the dumpsters are located and any security controls around them. It's likely they won't be under surveillance, but do take note of any bright lights, nearby entrances, foot traffic and proximity to vehicle traffic.

- **Guards** – Take photos of the guards, their tours and their badges. Determine if they're employed by a security guard agency or if they are employees of the building's management company.

- **Access Control Points** – Determine what access controls are required to access the building, such as: proximity cards, ID cards, PIN entry, turnstiles, mantraps, security cameras, motion detectors, lobbies, etc. Most security controls are placed in the front entrances while other entrances are equipped with far less security protection. But the goal here is to learn what security authorization points you *should* be going through. Later on, you can figure out how to bypass them.

- **Badges** – Take as many close up pictures of visitor badges and employee badges. It can sometimes be tricky to pull off. But having high-resolution images will do wonders for forging logos and bar codes.

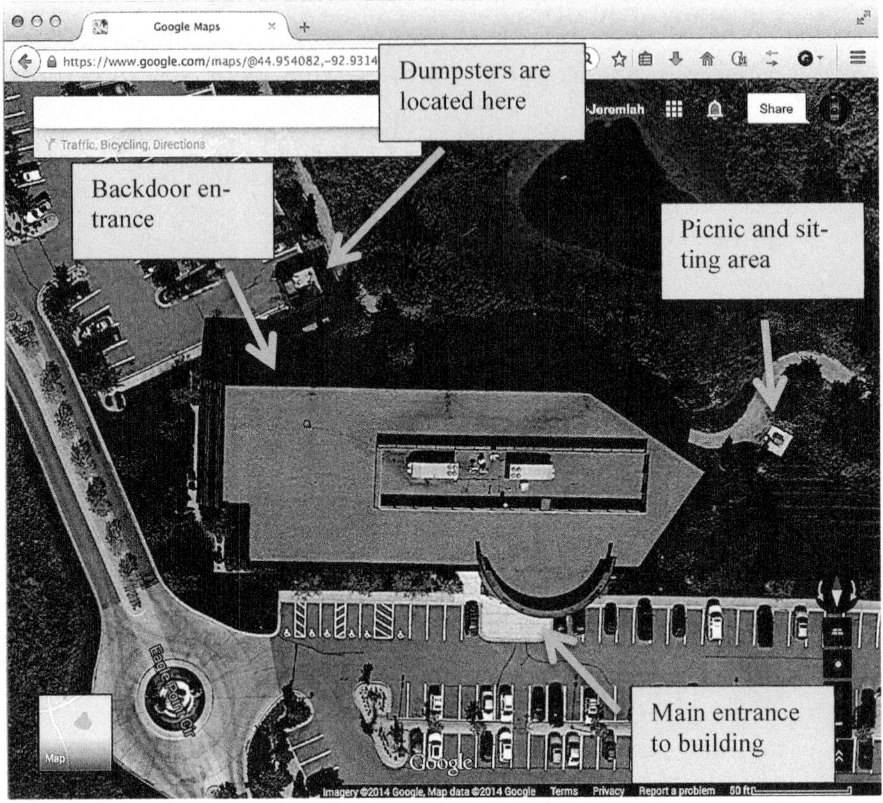

Google Earth aerial view of RedTeam Security's office building

Google Earth and Google Streetview are very useful tools for several reasons. They can be extremely valuable during the planning stages, from pretext planning to dumpster diving. Maps that Google Earth provides are also to scale, which simply adds even greater value. I personally make heavy use of Google Earth maps for planning purpose and through the pretexting phase.

Google Earth provides a social engineer with the capability to gain intelligence about the physical layout with little effort. The information captured from Google Earth will prove to be invaluable resource for social engineers during planning and execution. It also adds a layer of anonymity. The social engineer can leverage the data without having to covertly photograph them and potentially raise suspicion.

Covert photography is an important aspect of surveillance and information gathering. It is not your traditional photography, however. It involves going at it at a much different approach. First of all it is important to configure and use your camera in a way that won't let others on to what you're doing. I use a Canon Rebel XTI to shoot from my vehicle. It is an older digital SLR but it gets the job done in those situations. Personally, I recommend going with a digital camera with a smaller body but good zoom and auto focus features.

Taking covert photos doesn't give you much time to setup a shot. This is due to having to blend in or covertly sneak photos. Again, a camera that has good auto focus is paramount. Here are some key configurations for your digital camera:

- **Auto Focus** – The camera should support point and click use allowing for quick but clear snapshots

- **Flash** – This should be disabled for obvious reasons.

- **Auto ISO** – The camera should support automatic ISO mode so that it changes quickly relative to what is in focus.

- **Shutter Sounds / Beeps** – Configure the camera to be silent. In some cases this is not possible for some cameras. In situations where I need to be up close and quiet, I use a compact camera that doesn't click or beep.

One of my personal favorite cameras is the shirt button video recorder. The video camera's lens is situated in the center of the button and slips into your shirt in place of a button. The application for this camera is ideal for videotaping the inside of lobbies, shared office spaces, parking lots, etc. It can be used extensively to covertly identify where motion detectors and security cameras are placed without raising attention. With any luck, sometimes you can grab decent footage of badges.

Covert video recorder disguised as a shirt button

There are several adaptations of this camera for sale online and just about anyone will do. There are models that come with different styled and colored buttons to match your shirt. Other variations come inside backpacks, brief cases, watches and the list goes on. The video quality is not fantastic, but that's not the objective. It provides a more discreet way of obtaining information. The captured footage can then be reviewed and used to develop a more strategic social engineering plan.

Dumpster Diving

Now onto the least glamorous part of information gathering, dumpster diving. Dumpster diving is simply the process of going through the target's trash in an effort to uncover information, electronic media, or discarded documents that might be helpful in a social engineering test. Yes, it is a dirty and stinky job. But it's a dirty job that will reward you for your bravery. It is amazing what people throw away. Everything from computers, media storage equipment, USB drives and a treasure trove of paper documents. I like to call it, "dirty data."

It is the media storage devices and paper documents that social engineers are most interested in. And not necessarily the confidential paper documents either. Dirty data could simply be discarded invoices from the organization's IT services vendor or a discarded printout of telephone extensions. It may even be an old vacation schedule. Whatever it might be, these bits of dirty data should be snatched up and held onto as information.

More often than not, neither time nor the location will allow you to perform analysis on the trash onsite. So, what exactly should you take with you? Unless you have super powers that let you see through garbage bags, there is no great answer for that. The best advice is to take the lightest bags first. The trash in these bags usually comes from office waste paper baskets, so you're more likely to fair better in terms of gaining intelligence. But unfortunately, it tends to also be somewhat messy. Discarded coffee cups, napkins, wrappers and take out boxes will be mixed in.

Office cleaning staff usually makes their rounds of office/cubicle trash pickup all at the same time. This is advantageous since it means that trash similar in nature (paper documents) will likely be in the same bag. The contents may be somewhat evident as well (light, yet bulgy). Grab these bags first.

Dumpster diving is best performed in the late evening, so as not to stir up any suspicion from potential onlookers. And of course, before any dumpster diving begins, it should be well within the scope of the Rules of Engagement and legal in the state it's being performed.

A quick drive-by or aerial reconnaissance using Google Earth will help plan the travel route to and from the target location. Ideally, it should not take more than 10 minutes onsite. It should also involve at least two people working in tandem. For example, one person to jump inside the dumpster and toss trash out. The other person should load it into the vehicle and serve as a lookout. The entire process should be carried out as quickly as possible with the analysis portion to be conducted at an offsite location.

Dumpster diving truly is a dirty job. Thus, you need to be prepared to get dirty and take precautions so that you don't get injured. Remember, you will likely be up against broken glass, protruding nails and discarded furniture among other undesirables. For that reason and more, I recommend the following equipment:

- Step ladders
- Extra garbage bags
- Waist high waders (dark)
- Hand held flashlight and/or head worn lamp
- Safety glasses
- Steel toe reinforced boots
- Heavy duty gloves
- Thick long sleeve shirt and grubby jeans (dark)

- Change of clothes and garbage bag for your grubby clothes
- Vehicle with enough room to transport garbage bags and discarded items taken from the target location
- First-aid kit

But before getting your hands dirty, no pun intended, there must be a plan of attack. Before going onsite, there should be some plan or expectation of what information is being sought out. For example, discarded invoices and technical documents would be looked-for if the pretext was to be around pretending to be an IT service engineer. Ultimately, it's a crapshoot. You never know what you're going to find until you find it. You probably won't know what exactly are in the bags you're taking. It will likely be dark and you may not time to acquire everything you want. But having a high level plan will save time.

Making sense of the information collected is one of the most important steps in dumpster diving. Obviously, some pieces of information will be more valuable than others. To make the analysis process go efficiently, the following information should be sought out:

- **Letterhead paper** – It allows for making realistic forgeries, if necessary. It may also provide value in its content and give way of the names/titles of others in the org.

- **Invoices/Billing Info** – Useful for knowing who the target does business with and may help during pretexting.

- **Technical Documents** – Information about the infrastructure of the external/internal network configuration (IPs, networks, diagrams, OS, vendors).

- **Employee Information** – Information such as extension listings, cubicle maps and schedules. Useful for masquerading as an employee.

- **Emails** – Could be useful for their content, but would provide email address naming convention, email server technology and names of other individuals inside the org.

- **Electronic Media** – Floppy disks, CDs, DVDs, hard drives, USB drives. Extremely valuable in finding out information that is likely not available online or via other sources. A social engineer should acquire electronic media at every opportunity.

- **Shredded Documents** – These documents provide the most useful information. Most office shredders turn documents into long thin strips of paper. What's more, the shredded document is usually kept all in the same waste paper basket. As a result, typical office shredding is almost useless. Most office-shredded documents can be reconstructed.

Let's pause for a moment to discuss shredded documents since these documents are important. Typical office shredders do not do a good job of destroying documents. Instead, think of office shredders as a way of obfuscating the document. It makes is difficult to read, but does not make it unreadable.

Most office/home shredders slice in wide, long one-way shredding patterns leaving some text still readable. With time and effort, documents that have been shredded like this can be reconstructed by hand or with a little help from technology.

Shredded document showing long, wide remnants by a typical office shredder

The Unshredder (http://www.unshredder.com/) is a software application designed to reduce the time consumed by social engineers and investigators reconstructing shredded documents. The interface is rather intuitive and should not pose a significant learning curve for any computer savvy person. The software does require a flat bed scanner for reconstruction. At the time of this writing, it is a Windows-based application requiring about 1GB of RAM and about 1GB of free disk space. I've used the application with good results.

When considering reconstruction of shredded documents, the following options must be considered:

- How much time can I afford to devote toward reconstruction? Can I justify the time?
- How obscure are the shredded documents? Are they shredded strip-cut, cross-cut or micro-cut?
- Is there any legible text on the documents? Will my efforts produce valuable information?

The general rule of thumb before any considering reconstruction project is that there be at least two legible leads. That is, there should be shredded, but legible text, which triggers something of interest. It should garner enough interest that would justify hours of reconstruction work. If unable to piece together the first lead, you can fallback to the second lead and still attempt to gain something of value. Whatever the leads might be they should support the underlying social engineering plan and provide some level of value for the effort.

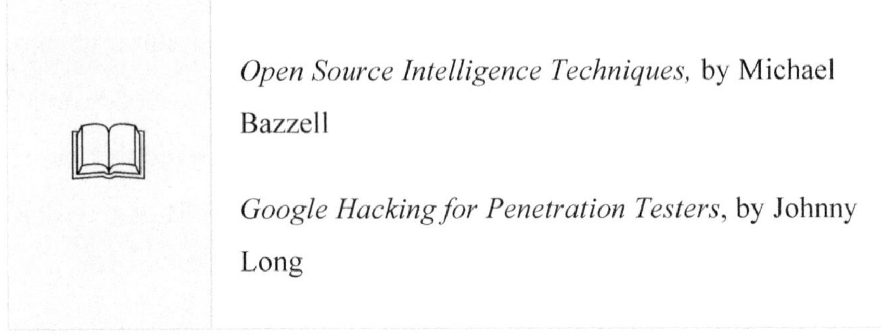

Open Source Intelligence Techniques, by Michael Bazzell

Google Hacking for Penetration Testers, by Johnny Long

Chapter 6:
Tools

Tools facilitate the efficient execution of social engineering tests and are an integrated part of the social engineering assessment process. In most cases, tools can spell the difference between success and failure. Many of the tactics and theories discussed in this book may be considered unethical in certain situations. For that reason, the tactics examined here should be used for ethical purposes only.

In this chapter, we will closely examine the many different types of tools available to the social engineer. These tools range in nature quite significantly depending upon the task at hand. Therefore, we will broadly discuss a sampling of tools from each of the main categories identified.

The following topics will be covered in this chapter:

- Computer Based Tools
- Physical Tools
- Telephone Tools

Computer Based Tools

As I stated earlier in this book, information gathering is paramount to a successful social engineering test. Just as a comprehensive information gathering strategy should involve multiple data sources, so too should a savvy social engineer leverage many information gathering tools. In general, tools give social engineers the capability to gather information far and wide with greater efficiency. Some of the tools we'll cover not only help search and gather intelligence, but also help execute tests as well.

Computer based tools are a category that used quite often. This is by no means a full and complete list, but the computer-based tools we will cover are the most commonly used ones.

Kali Linux

Kali Linux is a freely available security Linux distribution designed especially for penetration testing and digital forensics. Kali Linux comes preinstalled with well over 200 security tools and can be booted from a live CD, live USB drive or virtual machine. Why am I mentioning Kali Linux? Kali happens to come preinstalled with all of the computer based tools we are covering here as well as the tools mentioned in the previous chapter. Since social engineering testing is sometimes teamed together with red team testing, Kali makes a great one-stop shop Linux distro.

Kali Linux 1.0 is based on a derivative of Debian Wheezy. So, Debian fans will certainly enjoy the co-mingling of the two. I certainly do!

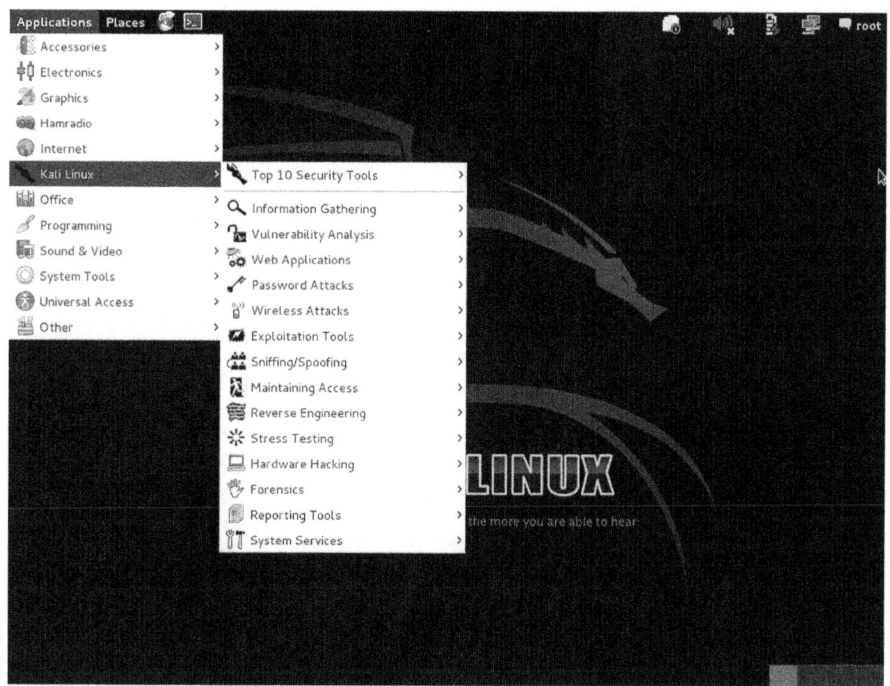

Screenshot of Kali Linux and the menu of preinstalled tools

Kali is the official successor of the former BackTrack security distribution. In fact, the very same group, Offensive Security, maintains it. The evolution of BackTrack, now retired, to Kali has been in the making for several years. As a security distribution overall, Kali Linux is the premiere security distribution and I recommend it for social engineering purposes. As an aside, I have been using BackTrack since its beta debut in 2006 and personally recommend its use as an all purpose Linux distribution as well.

Kali Linux can be downloaded at the following address: http://www.kali.org/downloads/

It is available for download by torrent or direct HTTP in 64-bit or 32-bit ISO image.

In short, Kali has a number of security tools that can be leveraged to gather information about your target beyond the tools we will discuss next. At the time of this writing, Kali has over 50 tools designed for information gathering purposes. Ultimately, the tools you will use will depend greatly upon the objectives of the social engineering test. However, there's a good chance Kali will have the tool you need for the project.

Social Engineering Toolkit (SET)

What would a social engineering book be without discussing the Social Engineering Toolkit? The Social Engineering Toolkit (SET) is specifically designed to perform some of the most advanced social engineering attacks. It is both an information-gathering tool and an exploitation tool. SET was created and written by David Kennedy, of TrustedSec fame. It is an open-source, freely available and written in

Python. Since its inception, it has become an industry standard with heavy support from the information security community.

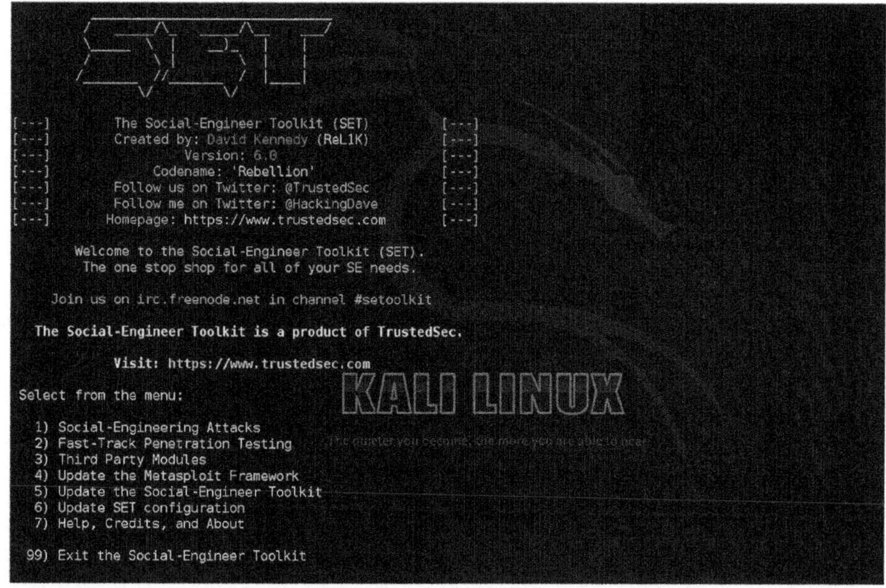

Screenshot of the Social Engineering Toolkit main menu

SET comes with an array of social engineering capabilities. These range from spear phishing, media drop infection to Arduino based attack vector. For the purposes of this book, we are most concerned with SET's spear phishing attacks, infectious media generator and its mass mailer attack. While there are other features of the toolkit that are most valuable, these three features are some of the most commonly used.

Before we go any further, it's worth mentioning that SET comes integrated with the Metasploit Framework. This is evident from SET's main menu of options. The Metasploit Framework is an open source framework for developing and executing exploit code. We will discuss Metasploit in a little more detail coming up next.

The Social Engineering Toolkit comes preinstalled on the Kali Linux distribution. Alternatively, it can be obtained through Git via the following:

```
git clone
https://github.com/trustedsec/social-
engineer
```

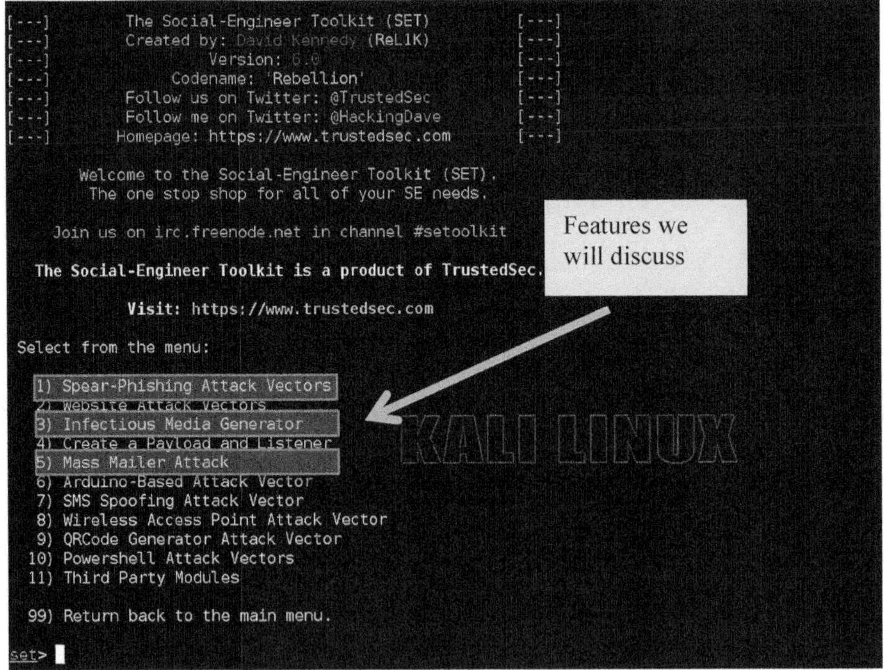

Screenshot of SET's *Social Engineering Attacks* sub-menu

SET features a great set of options all around. What is great about SET is that its modules add capability for generating payloads and starting listeners with testing. This is in part due to the integration with Metasploit, which we will get to next. This integration allows you to specifically craft email messages and send them to a large or small number of people with attached malicious file payloads and corresponding listeners. To help get started, SET provides a wizard to assist in the design and execution.

We will concentrate on the Social Engineering Attacks, option #1, from the SET main menu. The list of features in the Social Engineering Attacks sub-menu gives us a set of 12 options. For the purposes of this book, we will discuss the following items from the SET Social Engineering Attacks sub-menu:

- Spear-Phishing Attack Vectors (menu option #1)
- Infectious Media Generator (menu option #3)
- Mass Mailer Attack (menu option #5)

Spear-Phishing Attack Vectors

When selecting option #1, Spear-Phishing Attack Vectors from the main menu. You are presented with 3 menu options. The options are as follows: 1) Perform a Mass Email Attack, 2) Create a File Format Payload and 3) Create a Social-Engineering Template.

```
   1) Perform a Mass Email Attack
   2) Create a FileFormat Payload
   3) Create a Social-Engineering Template

  99) Return to Main Menu

set:phishing>
```

Screenshot of SET's *Spear-Phishing Attack Vectors* sub-menu

Option #1 is a wizard driven menu that walks the user through selecting a file format for the exploit (e.g. Adobe PDF with embedded EXE). The wizard goes on to help setup a payload that is launched once the user opens the file (e.g.: Windows Meterpreter Reverse_TCP). The wizard then helps the user add content and finally sends the email out.

Option #2 in this sub-menu is a manual approach toward option #1 for the expert user. Option #3 allows the user to develop and save spear phishing email content to be re-used in the future. This is especially helpful if you use consistently spear phish and use SET to do so.

Infectious Media Generator

Another great feature to the Social Engineering Toolkit is the Infectious Media Generator for USB/CD/DVD media. This SET module allows the user to create an `autorun.inf` and a corresponding Metasploit payload. When the media is inserted, it will automatically run and execute the Metasploit payload, if the autorun feature is enabled. There are many Metasploit payloads to choose from. However, the Meterpreter payload is the most common and offers a great deal of control (e.g.: persistent backdoor).

```
Pick the attack vector you wish to use: fileformat bugs or a straight executable.

   1) File-Format Exploits
   2) Standard Metasploit Executable

  99) Return to Main Menu

set:infectious>
```

Screenshot of the *Infectious Media Generator* sub-menu

The Infectious Media Generator feature is especially useful for Baiting targets. USB drives containing payloads are often placed on the ground in public areas near the target location. The USB drives are labeled with interesting titles, such as "payroll" or "private pics." The strategy is designed to spark the user's curiosity and increase the chances of the user plugging the device into their computer.

Mass Mailer Attack

```
   What do you want to do:

    1.  E-Mail Attack Single Email Address
    2.  E-Mail Attack Mass Mailer

    99. Return to main menu.

set:mailer>
```

Screenshot of the *Mass Mailer Attack* sub-menu

SET's Mass Mailer Attack feature is very straightforward, but handy. Most traditional email programs don't always allow the user to send email to a large number of recipients. The E-Mail Attack Mass Mailer provides the user with an easy way to import a text file of email recipients in just a few taps. Alternatively, option #1 can be used to send a one-off email or to simply test email delivery using your own SMTP relay host.

Metasploit Framework

The Metasploit Framework is an open source, freely available security project. It is a tool for developing and executing exploit code. There are smaller sub projects that come with the Framework worth noting and include: the Opcode database, shellcode archive, MSF Encoder, etc.

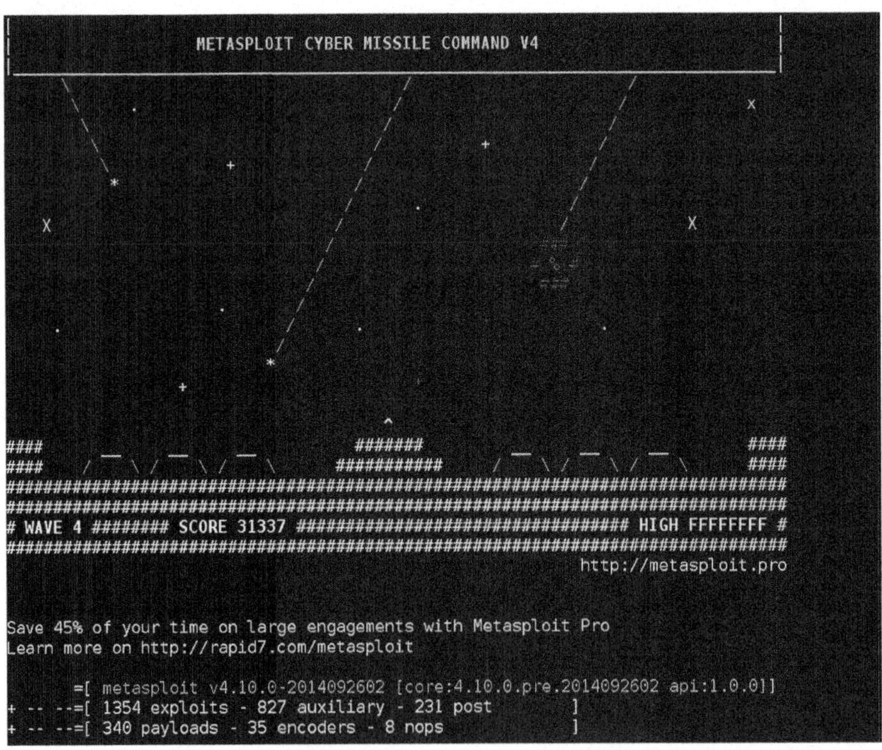

Screenshot the Metasploit console running in the command-line version (msfconsole)

Metasploit has a number of modules that users can leverage in order to exploit and compromise systems. At the time of this writing, Metasploit has 1,354 exploits, 340 payloads and 35 encoders. Metasploit also comes with auxiliary programs as well. These auxiliary programs do not necessarily involve the exploitation of services or hosts, they're auxiliary programs that do specialized tasks. For instance, there are Metasploit auxiliary programs that do fuzzing, scanning, denial-of-service and more.

The Metasploit Framework can be downloaded for free at the following URL: http://www.rapid7.com/products/metasploit/metasploit-community-registration.jsp

It runs on Unix, Windows and Mac OS X and can be integrated to run with Nmap, Nexpose and Nessus. Alternatively, Metasploit comes preinstalled on the Kali Linux security distribution.

Since Metasploit's inception in 2003 by HD Moore, it has undergone several changes over the years. Today, a security company called, Rapid7, now owns Metasploit. As a result of the Rapid7 acquisition in 2009, there are multiple versions of Metasploit including commercial paid-for versions. The commercial versions of Metasploit are geared toward teams and often involve additional feature sets.

Breakdown of Metasploit versions:

- **Metasploit Framework** – The free version. It consists of the command line interface.
- **Metasploit Community Edition** – This is also free, and includes a web-based interface.
- **Metasploit Express** – An open-core commercial edition intended for security teams that includes a web-based GUI and some of the Pro features, such as smart brute forcing and automated evidence collection.
- **Metasploit Pro** – An open-core commercial edition that includes all features of Metasploit Express, plus web application scanning/exploitation, social engineering campaigns and VPN pivoting.

Metasploit Pro comes with powerful social engineering campaign features. At the time of this writing, this feature is quite similar to what SET does. For that reason, we won't go into any further detail on its capabilities here. Having said that, the team at Rapid7 is constantly improving the product. So, I urge you to give it a try and see if it suits your needs. A fully functional 14-day trial can be acquired for Metasploit Pro by following this link:

http://www.rapid7.com/products/metasploit/metasploit-pro-registration.jsp

Maltego

Maltego is an open source intelligence tool (OSINT) and forensics application provided by Paterva. Maltego provides the user with a library of transforms for discovery of data from open sources. It allows for the visualization of information in a graphical format for link analysis and data mining.

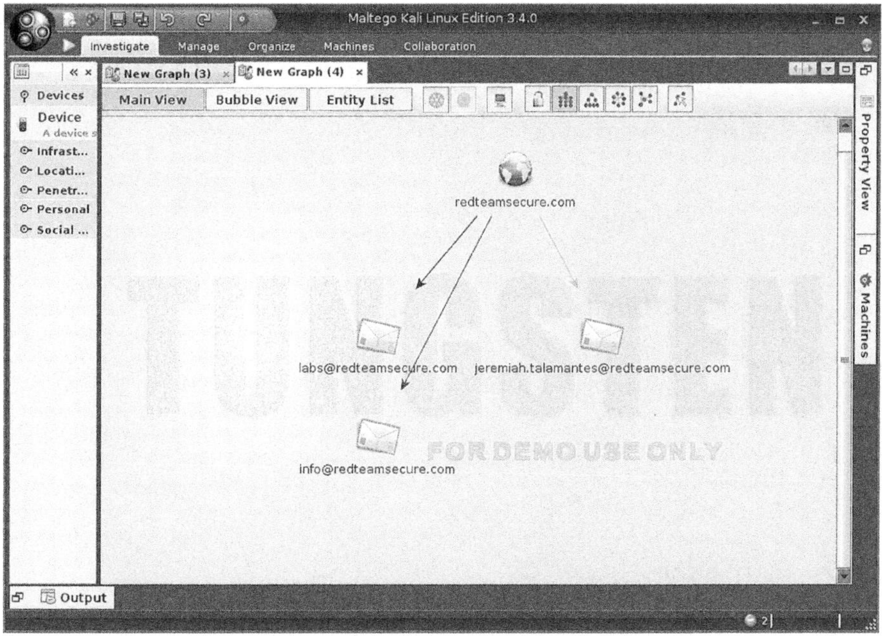

Screenshot of Maltego running on Kali Linux

At its core, Maltego focuses on analyzing real-world relationships between people, groups, websites, domains, networks, Internet infrastructure and affiliations, such as Twitter and Facebook.

Maltego can be used to determine relationships and real world links between:

- People
- Groups (social networks)
- Companies
- Organizations
- Web sites
- Internet infrastructure
    - Domains
    - DNS names
    - Netblocks and IP addresses
- Phrases
- Affiliations
- Documents and files

A free community version of Maltego comes preinstalled on Kali Linux. While the free community edition works wonderfully, there are some limitations.

To get the most out of Maltego, the commercial version is recommended.

In essence, Maltego can be used to efficiently gather information for social engineering purposes. The graphical user interface helps visually display relationships and aggregate information from sources all over the Internet – even if they are three or four degrees of separation away.

Maltego is available for download by following this link: http://www.paterva.com/web6/products/download2.php

Physical Tools

No social engineer's tool bag would be complete without an assortment of physical tools. These tools can aid a tester in gathering information through surveillance and even through exploitation. For this section, we will discuss a few different categories of physical tools. A good social engineer should know how and when to utilize these tools to achieve the best results.

Cameras

We discussed cameras briefly in Chapter 5. Cameras are very useful tools for social engineers when it becomes necessary to visually capture and record information swiftly.

Photography equipment and tactics in the social engineering world is vastly different from those of the hobbyist photographer. Instead, there are several factors that differ greatly. First and foremost are the objective and the approach. Photographic surveillance almost always happens very quickly and often discreetly. As a result, there isn't much time to frame and focus a shot. These factors play heavily into the social engineer's methodology and their equipment choices.

Form Factor

The right camera equipment for the job arrives in many different forms. One of the most significant for the social engineer is the camera's size. Most photos end up to be quick and dirty shots from the hip, not to mention discreet. Lugging around a camera with a big body, like some digital SLRs, would not be consistent with trying to be inconspicuous. Size matters.

To add a bit more complexity, *some* photos actually can be framed and focused. These types of shots are usually long distance surveillance in nature. One example of this type of surveillance might be used to gather information about the physical exterior of a building while being taken from inside a vehicle in the parking lot. In these situations, distance plays a significant role in the selection of camera equipment.

I recommend having at least two distinct cameras. Overall, their general purpose is for long distance surveillance opportunities and shoot from the hip covert/stealthy shots. See the table below for a couple of recommendations.

Distance and short-range camera recommendations:

	Panasonic Lumix DMC-TZ40	**Olympus Stylus SP-100**
Range	Good	Superb!
Noise	Quiet	"Clicky"
Body	Slim Easy to conceal	Large Difficult to conceal
Color	Black	Black
Quality	Excellent (18 MP)	Excellent (16 MP)
Application	Close-up Covert Surveillance	Long-range Distance Surveillance

Panasonic Lumix DMC-TZ40

Olympus Stylus SP-100

Covert Surveillance

Video

Covert video surveillance is ideal for information gathering when "casing the joint," as they say. This allows the social engineer with the capability to record their surroundings without having to rely on memory alone. Captured footage can be reviewed at a later date to identify security controls, such as cameras and motion detectors. Footage can also be reviewed to measure distance as well as find other notable items of interest not initially discovered.

Thanks to the emergence of the "nanny cam" in recent years, there has been surge of covert cameras and listening devices on the market. These stealthy devices are capable of capturing and storing audio and video via cable or by wireless transmitter. They are often secretly housed in everyday household items, such as: teddy bears, clocks, vases and books.

Today, covert cameras can be found hidden inside items that are more germane to the corporate office world. In fact, there's even been exponential growth in technology toward body-worn cameras. The application of body-worn cameras is almost limitless. There are so many to choose from and can be found readily available online. It is these types of cameras that provide the social engineer with the best possible results.

A well-equipped social engineer will have several covert cameras from which to use at any given time. Having a variety will enable the social engineer to respond quickly and effectively without giving away his or her motives. The table below represents a list of recommended cameras and their applications.

Recommended "must have" covert cameras:

	Button Cam	**Glasses Cam**	**Bag Cam**	**Pen Cam**
Video	Excellent	Excellent	Excellent	Good
Audio	Good	Good	Good	Good
Video Quality	720x480	720x480	HD	HD
Application	Up-close	Distance	Distance	Up-close
Usage	Ideal for video at chest height (badges, door locks)	Ideal for recording faces and physical controls (cameras, detectors)	Ideal for video at waist height and lower. Great recording for interior lay-outs and measuring dis-tances walked	Ideal for re-cording keystrokes or simply re-cording audio

Glasses camera

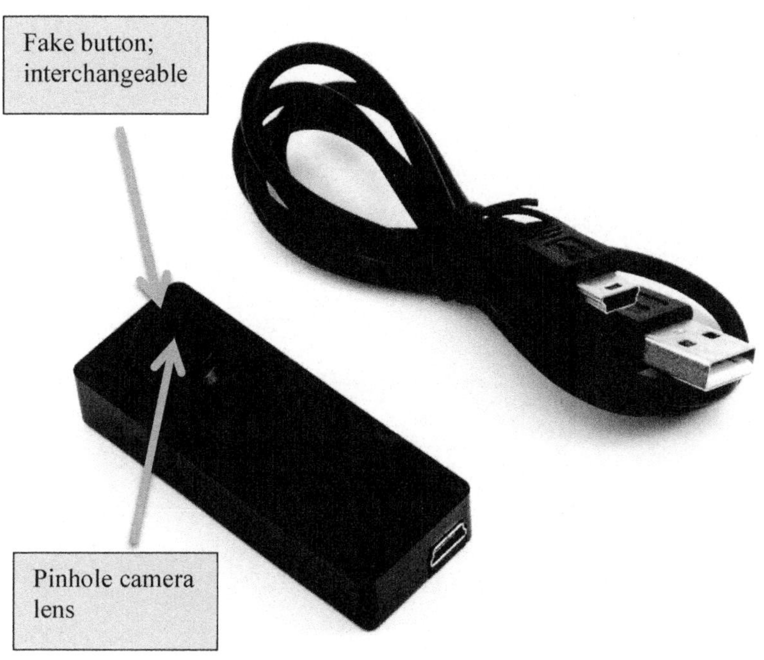

Button camera with USB cable

Pen camera

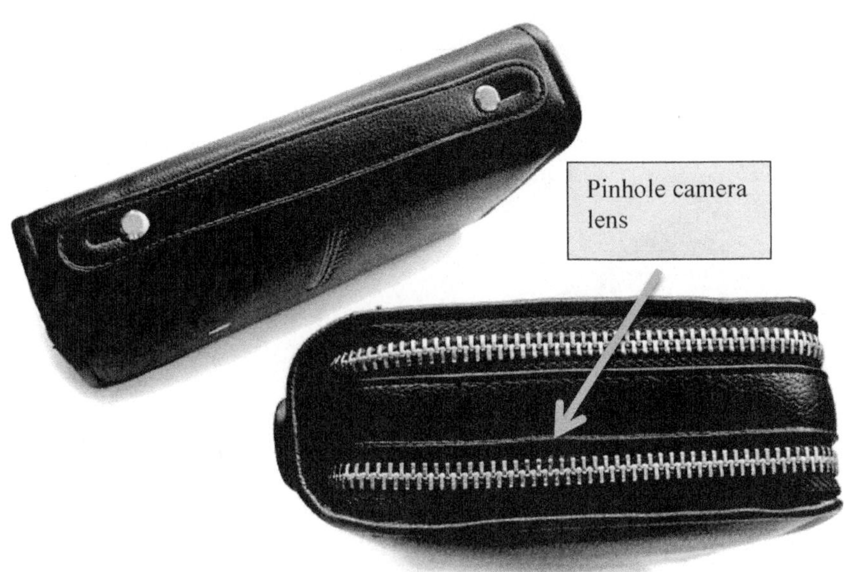

Bag camera

The covert cameras shown here are by no means the best or the only ones you'll need. Different pretexts and tests will call for different equipment. However, these cameras are generic and all-purpose enough to be used during several pretexts.

Audio

Sometimes a social engineering test calls for the gathering of audio information. Perhaps, the goal of the test is to place a bug in the executive boardroom. Or maybe the test calls for a less complex approach. For simple applications, the pen camera is small and inconspicuous enough to satisfy these scenarios. However, for more involved or live-streaming needs, a more sophisticated configuration may be required.

For real-time monitoring of audio, a radio transmitting audio device is ideal. An all-purpose solution can be easily acquired online. See this link:
http://www.newegg.com/Product/Product.aspx?Item=9SIA2C51B21722&nm_mc=KNC-GoogleMKP&cm_mmc=KNC-GoogleMKP-_-pla-_-Wireless+Surveillance-_-9SIA2C51B21722

This kit contains a wireless audio bug that is powered by a 9-volt battery. The kit includes an FM receiver and earphones. The bug can provide about 1 to 3 days of remote audio, depending upon the quality of the battery. The signal can be picked up from about 200 to 300 meters away depending upon obstructions.

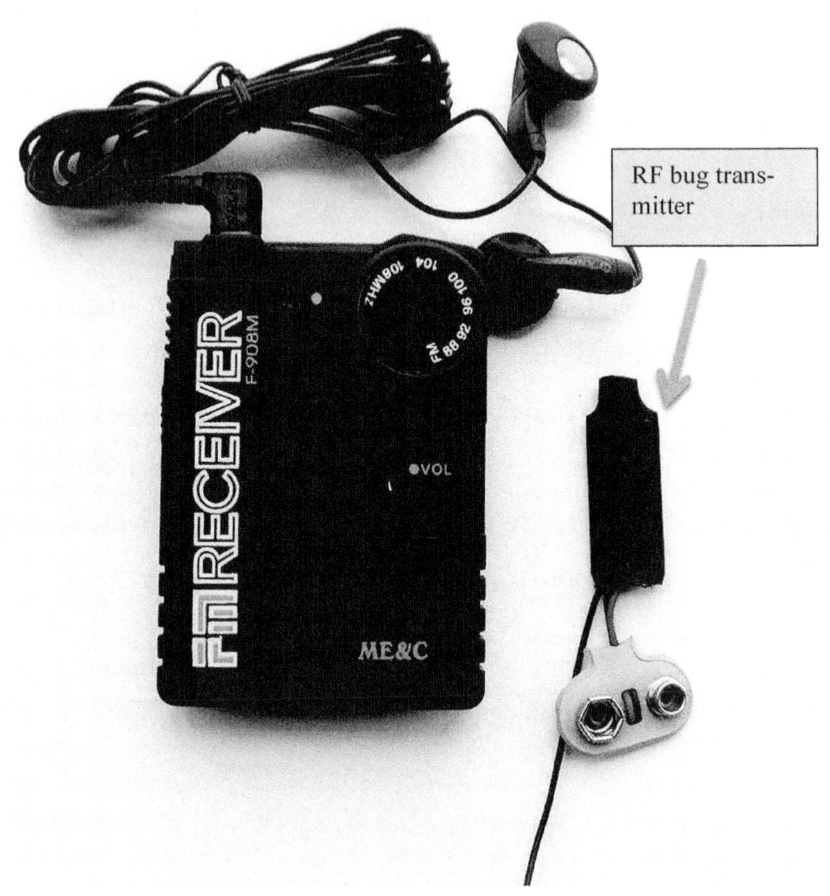

Wireless bug covert RF FM kit – Receiver, headphones, audio bug transmitter with 9v battery attachment

At the time of this writing, I have yet to upgrade from this kit. It works wonderfully for the everyday average complexity engagements. Therefore, I recommend this solution as an entry-level solution. For tests involving greater distances, longer listening time, greater clarity and greater security, a more professional solution would be required.

GPS

GPS vehicle tracking allows for the monitoring and routing of a target's whereabouts. There could be several use cases where the need to map a target's route is needed. For example, it may be necessary to learn about the target's route to and from work. Using this device, a social engineer may be able to learn where the target often goes to lunch or spends their happy hour. All of this is important and useful information from which to leverage during a social engineering test.

Magnetic GPS tracker with USB interface

This tracking device is ultra-compact and easy to conceal in the undercarriage of a vehicle. Its powerful magnet will ensure it stays put. The target's route can be displayed over a satellite image via Google Earth.

This device can be found here: http://www.proofpronto.com/gps-tracking-key.html

One important item to note is that this particular GPS tracker does not provide real-time GPS information. Therefore, you must install it and later retrieve it in order to obtain routing information. It will simply plug into any USB port running on any Windows-based OS. If your test requires real-time GPS tracking, there are other more expensive GPS trackers that will do the job.

Before engaging in GPS tracking of any individual, it must first be agreed upon with the client and fall well within the Rules of Engagement. Observe any local or state legal requirements as well.

Clothing

Having the right apparel is crucial. We discussed this in previous chapters. Social engineers must fly under the radar and not stand out in any way. The key is to blend in and not draw any attention. Depending upon the occasion, there may be several clothing requirements. They are too numerous to mention here. But the following list is designed to be an all-purpose recommendation for social engineers.

The following table is a recommendation for building out your social engineering closet. It is by no means an all-inclusive list, but should be extensive enough to satisfy a number of engagement scenarios. A portion of this list has been repeated from the Dumpster Diving section in the previous chapter.

Business casual outfit	Formal business attire (suit)	“Casual Friday” attire	Grubby jeans, dark
Long-sleeve, thick, dark shirt	Steel toe, work boots	Heavy duty work gloves	Dark colored baseball hat
Sunglasses	Khakis	Polo shirt	Waist high waders

The previous table may seem somewhat simplistic. But, these items have been in my social engineering wardrobe for many years. Along the way, I managed to pick up a few single use items, like a lab coat and a hardhat. Those engagements will come and go and you can’t necessarily start off and assemble a wardrobe to prepare for them. However, having some semblance of stock wardrobe will make social engineering go a little smoother.

Telephone

When you call a target during a social engineering excursion, you don’t want to be identified by your number and maybe not even your voice. There are several easy ways to spoof your number and mask your voice. The SpoofCard application is an IOS and Android app for smart phones that will spoof your number, change your voice, record the call and even add convincing background noise.

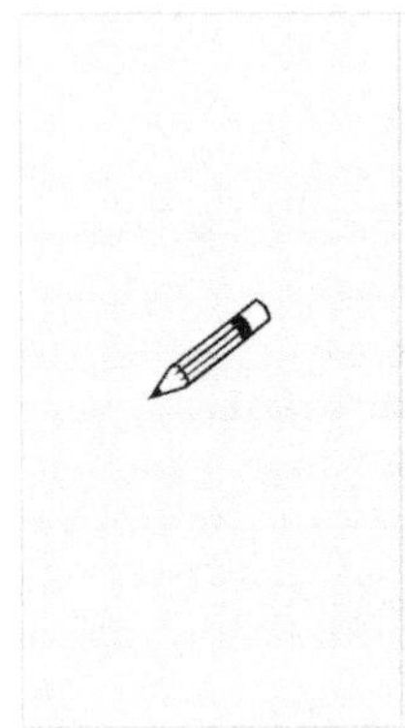

The SpoofCard mobile app for smart phones can be downloaded by following this link: https://www.spoofcard.com/apps

SpoofCard is a for-pay commercial application with relatively reasonable package pricing.

Lock Picking

Lock picking is often associated with social engineering, red teaming and physical penetration testing. The topic is far too vast to be adequately covered here. However, there are countless online resources dedicated to the subject matter. Additionally, there are a number of books about lock picking as well. My advice is to follow the resources that will do it proper justice.

Bump Keys

As any lock picker would say, lock picking is a learned skill that takes time and a lot of practice. Having said that, there are some "shortcuts" on the market. Bump keys can aid an unskilled individual in the process of picking locks. While they may be useful, they should not be used as the only approach for picking locks. Instead, one should take the time to develop the skill over time and practice.

Lock picking may cause irreparable damage, so be sure this tactic is approved under the Rules of Engagement.

More information on locking picking and bump keys can be found by following these links: http://toool.us/ and http://acehackware.com/collections/bump-keys

Miscellaneous Tools

This section will outline some miscellaneous tools a social engineer can use during any number of tests. This is a collection of some very useful tools that I use often and some that I wish I had.

Keylogger

The USB keylogger is a useful piece of equipment that simply plugs inline between the keyboard and the computer. Like the name says, it captures and stores keystrokes. Keystrokes can later be downloaded once the device is retrieved.

USB keylogger

VideoGhost

VideoGhost is similar to a Keylogger, it is a peripheral connection but instead it takes screen captures and stores the images on a ROM chip inside the connector.

Recording Night Vision Goggles

The name says it all. Great night vision capabilities with recording function to assist with information gathering/surveillance.

Covert Spy Cap

This records high-resolution video up to 1080P HD.

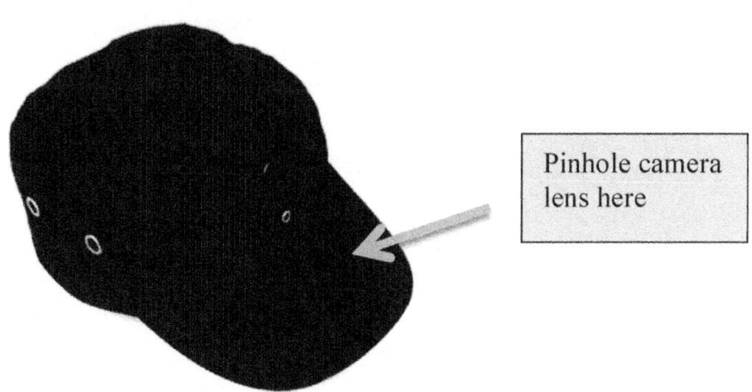

Lock Pick Gun (Snap Gun)

A lock pick gun is a tool that can be used to force open a lock without using the key. In some situations, it can be used to open a lock quicker than traditional lock picking but is more like to damage the lock.

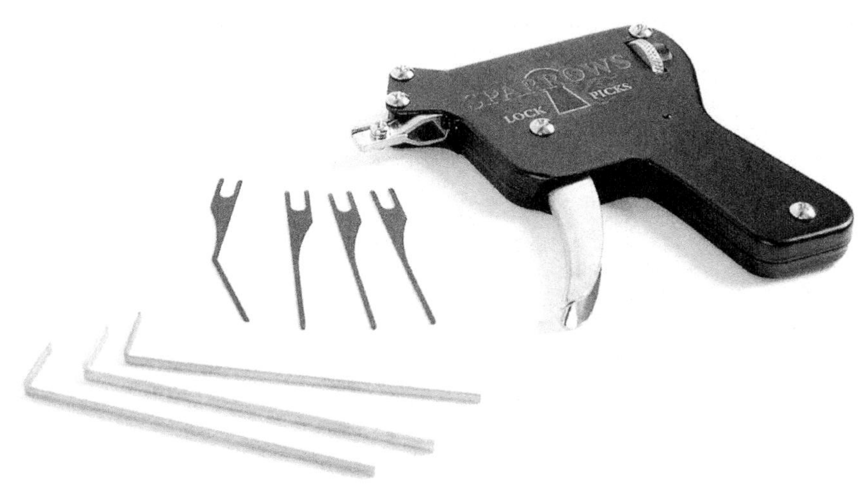

Practical Lock Picking, Second Edition: A Physical Penetration Tester's Training Guide, by Devian Ollam

Incognito Toolkit, by Rob Robideau

Unathorised Access: Physical Penetration Testing for IT Security Teams, by Wil Allsopp

Chapter 7: The Playbook

Due to its creative element and limitless opportunities, pretexting is one of the most fascinating forms of social engineering. Many of the tactics and theories discussed in this book may be considered unethical in certain situations. For that reason, the tactics examined here should be used for ethical purposes only.

In this chapter, we'll examine several tactics used by social engineers to manipulate targets through the fabrication of invented scenarios, known as pretexts. We will cover some of the most common pretexting tactics and learn through research and planning exercises.

The following plays will be covered in this chapter:

- Spear phishing
- Telephone
- Baiting
- Physical

Legal & Warranty Disclaimer

THE CONTENT IN THIS BOOK IS NOT INTENDED FOR ILLEGAL OR UNETHICAL PURPOSES. PRIOR TO MAKING USE OF THIS INFORMATION IN ANY FORM OR FASHION, FIRST CONSULT WITH ALL APPLICABLE LOCAL, STATE AND FEDERAL LAWS TO ENSURE LEGAL COMPLIANCE.

NEITHER THE PUBLISHER NOR THE AUTHOR SHALL BE LIABLE FOR DAMAGES ARISING HEREFROM. THE FACT THAT AN ORGANIZATION OR WEB SITE IS REFERRED TO IN THIS WORK AS A CITATION, SOURCE OR OTHERWISE DOES NOT MEAN THAT THE AUTHOR OR PUBLISHER ENDORSES THE INFORMATION THE ORGANIZER OF THE WEB SITE MAY PROVIDE OR RECOMMENDATIONS IT MAY MAKE.

THE PUBLISHER AND THE AUTHOR MAKE NO REPRESENTATIONS OR WARRANTIES WITH RESPECT TO THE ACCURACY OF COMPLETENESS OF THE CONTENTS OF THIS WORK AND SPECIFICALLY DISCLAIM ALL WARRANTIES OF FITNESS FOR A PARTICULAR PURPOSE. NO WARRANTY MAY BE CREATED OR EXTENDED BY SALES OR PROMOTIONAL MATERIALS. THE ADVICE AND STRATEGIES CONTAINED HEREIN MAY NOT BE SUITABLE FOR EVERY SITUATION. THIS WORK IS SOLD WITH THE UNDERSTANDING THAT THE PUBLISHER IS NOT ENGAGED IN RENDERING LEGAL, ACCOUNTING OR OTHER PROFESSIONAL SERVICES.

Spear Phishing

Phishing attacks cast a wide net and attempt to reel in as many victims as possible, while spear phishing attacks are targeted attacks pointed directly at either a company, industry or even specific people. This next section will focus on spear phishing pretext tactics.

Security Bulletin!	
Objective	To assess the target's adherence toward policy forbidding the opening of file attachments within email
Description	This is a very basic attack designed to get a target or targets to open a malicious file that will open a reverse shell payload to your listening server
Prerequisites	• Knowledge of the target e-mail address(es)
Tools & Equipment	• SMTP relay server • Social Engineer Toolkit (SET) • Metasploit Framework • Internet facing server for reverse shell listening connectivity

Play	1. Launch SET, select *Social Engineering Attacks -> Spear-Phishing Attack Vector ->* then select *Perform a Mass Email Attack* 2. Select *Adobe PDF Embedded EXE Social Engineering* and opt for the built-in BLANK PDF, then select the *Windows Reverse TCP Shell* 3. Enter your IP address for the payload listener and the listening port (443) 4. Use the following FROM address: *security.bulletin@microsoft.com* 5. Use the e-mail subject: *Critical Microsoft Security Bulletin* 6. Use the e-mail content: *Dear Microsoft Customer* *You are receiving this message because you are using Genuine Microsoft Software and your e-mail address has been subscribed to the Microsoft Windows Update mailing list.* *A highly critical security vulnerability has appeared in the wild and was reported for the first time <DATE>. The vulnerability affects all Microsoft Windows machines and allows an attacker to take full control of the vulnerable computer.*

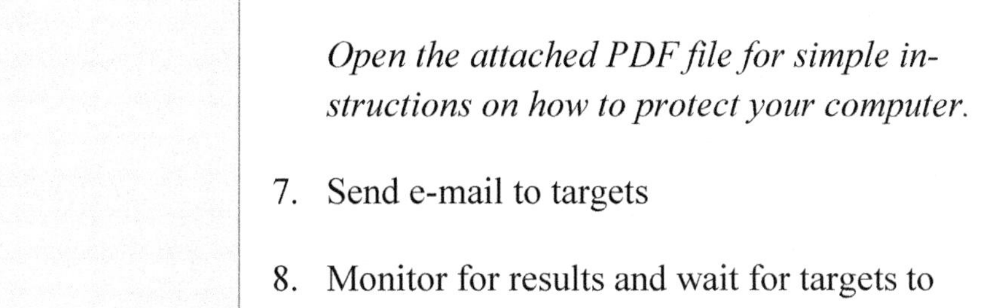

	Open the attached PDF file for simple instructions on how to protect your computer. 7. Send e-mail to targets 8. Monitor for results and wait for targets to connect.

Bank Security Email Alert	
Objective	To assess the target's adherence toward policy forbidding the opening of file attachments within email
Description	This pretext is a slightly different spin on a classic phishing test. But, we are not attempting to acquire banking information. The objective is to get the target to open a malicious file that will open a reverse shell payload to your listening server.
Prerequisites	• Knowledge of the target email address • Knowledge of the target's bank. This may be learned through surveillance, dumpster diving or GPS tracking.
Tools & Equipment	• SMTP relay server • Social Engineer Toolkit (SET) • Metasploit Framework • Internet facing server for reverse shell listening connectivity

Play	1. Launch SET, select *Social Engineering Attacks -> Spear-Phishing Attack Vector ->* then select *Perform a Mass Email Attack* 2. Select *Adobe PDF Embedded EXE Social Engineering* and opt for the built-in BLANK PDF, then select the *Windows Reverse TCP Shell* 3. Enter your IP address for the payload listener and the listening port (443) 4. Use the following FROM address: *fraud@[bankdomain.com]* 5. Use the email subject: *Suspicious Account Activity* 6. Use the email content: *Dear Customer* *You are receiving this message because you are a current [bank name] customer.* *Our Fraud & Prevention department has noted several suspicious transactions on your account originating from multiple overseas merchants. Our policy states that we require your assistance in determining the legitimacy of any suspicious charges totaling over $10,000. Please see the instructions below.*

	1). Open the attached PDF file for a detailed summary of each suspicious transaction. *2). Review each suspicious transaction shown along with the merchant, date and transaction amount.* *3). Validate any transactions as suspicious or unknown to the best of your ability. Denote all/any charges you wish to dispute.* *Your information is very important to us. We appreciate your cooperation. A representative will be contacting you shortly regarding this matter. Please reference incident number: FRDR-2039423990* 7. Send email to target 8. Monitor for results and wait for target to connect.

IRS Audit Notice	
Objective	To assess the target's adherence toward policy forbidding the opening of file attachments within email
Description	The objective is to get the target to open a malicious file that will open a reverse shell payload to your listening server.
Prerequisites	• Knowledge of the target email address
Tools & Equipment	• SMTP relay server • Social Engineer Toolkit (SET) • Metasploit Framework • Internet facing server for reverse shell listening connectivity
Play	1. Launch SET, select *Social Engineering Attacks -> Spear-Phishing Attack Vector ->* then select *Perform a Mass Email Attack* 2. Select *Adobe PDF Embedded EXE Social Engineering* and opt for the built-in BLANK PDF, then select the *Windows Re-*

	verse TCP Shell 3. Enter your IP address for the payload listener and the listening port (443) 4. Use the following FROM address: *notice@irs.gov* 5. Use the email subject: *Selected for IRS Audit* 6. Use the following pretext content: *Why are you receiving this notice?* *The tax information we have on file does not match the entries for [year]. A significant discrepancy has been discovered requiring your immediate cooperation.* *What steps should you take?* *In order to comply wit this audit notice, you must carry out the following steps:* *1). Open the attached PDF file for more information regarding the tax discrepancy matter.* *2). Print the document and keep for your records.* *A representative will be contacting you*

	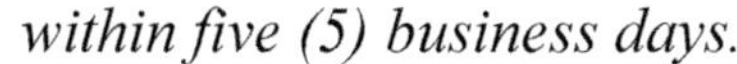 *within five (5) business days.* 7. *Send email to target* 8. *Monitor for results and wait for target to connect.*

Get Your Updates Here	
Objective	To assess the target's adherence toward policy visiting unknown web sites
Description	The objective is to get the target to visit a web site that is designed to "backdoor" their browser and potentially allow for various levels of system compromise. In this pretext, the social engineer is pretending (spoofing) to be a technical support person from the target's IT department or IT service provider. The objective is to entice targets to visit a malicious web site in order to "register" their computer to receive automatic security updates. For obvious reasons, the company's IT resources should not be included in the email recipient list. Rather, this pretext should be directed at less-technically savvy individuals who are more likely to fall victim.
Prerequisites	• Knowledge of the target email address • Knowledge of the target's email signature

Tools & Equipment	• Kali Linux (Highly recommended) • BeEF – Browser Exploitation Framework. (Preinstalled in Kali Linux or http://beefproject.com/) • Phony website purporting to be a SaaS security update delivery organization (see: http://www.securityupdatedelivery.com/) • See here for cheap web site templates: https://creativemarket.com/templates/websites • A convincing domain name • A web host provider
Play	1. Invent a name for the phony SaaS security company 2. Register a domain name for your phony company. Optionally, you may elect to the make the domain name a "private" registration. 3. Procure a web-hosting provider (e.g.: Dreamhost) if you do not already have one. 4. Become acquainted with BeEF: https://www.youtube.com/user/TheBeefproject 5. Install BeEF on an externally facing web

server. Or, use the BeEF that comes preinstalled on Kali Linux (recommended).

6. Use the following FROM address:

   spoofedemail@[targetdomainname]

7. Use or adapt the following email subject:

   Action Required: Security Update Registration

8. Adapt the following email pretext to your liking:

   All,

   To help better secure our company computers, we will begin using a service designed to download and install security updates on our systems automatically.

   Please click the link below and register your computer for updates by entering your name and email address on this site.

   Visit this website:
   [yourphonycompanydomainname]

   Thanks,
   [spoofed IT individual]

	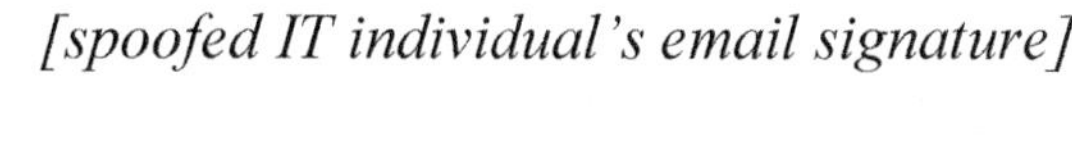 *[spoofed IT individual's email signature]* 9. Send email to target 10. Monitor for the BeEF console for results and wait for target to connect.

Company Re-Org	
Objective	To assess the target's adherence toward policy forbidding the opening of file attachments within email
Description	The objective is to get the target to open a malicious file that will open a reverse shell payload to your listening server. In this pretext, the social engineer is pretending (spoofing) to be a human resources person from the company's administration department. The goal behind this pretext is to entice targets to open an email attachment in order to be briefed on a "significant" company re-organization. For optimum results, the company's human resources staff should not be included in the email recipient list.
Prerequisites	• Knowledge of the target email address • Knowledge of one or more executive or management individuals
Tools & Equipment	• SMTP relay server

	• Social Engineer Toolkit (SET) • Metasploit Framework • Internet facing server for reverse shell listening connectivity
Play	1. Launch SET, select *Social Engineering Attacks -> Spear-Phishing Attack Vector ->* then select *Perform a Mass Email Attack* 2. Select *Adobe PDF Embedded EXE Social Engineering* and opt for the built-in BLANK PDF, then select the *Windows Reverse TCP Shell* 3. Enter your IP address for the payload listener and the listening port (443) 4. Use the following FROM address: *HR@[targetdomain.com]* 5. Use the email subject: *Company-wide Reorganization* 6. Use the following email content: *[Company name] has experienced significant change in recent months. In an effort to meet the demands of our industry, we must respond and adapt accordingly.* *As of [date] we will initiate a company-*

	wide reorganization of all groups/departments. In certain situations, this may result in the consolidation of certain departments. In other scenarios, some groups/departments may be transitioned. *For more information regarding this initiative, please refer to the details outlined in the attached file.* 7. Send email to targets 8. Monitor for results and wait for target to connect.

Telephone

Telephone is a social engineering attack conducted over the telephone in an effort to get the target to divulge information or persuade them into performing an action. According to statistics, those outside of the United States perform this type of social engineering often. It is certainly one of the most widely used forms of social engineering.

The Forgetful User	
Objective	To assess the targets susceptibility toward performing privileged actions without properly authenticating the user or divulging confidential information
Description	This is a classic social engineering pretext. In this maneuver, the social engineer telephones the organization's user Help Desk while purporting to be a legitimate user. The pretext is that the user has forgotten his/her network password or VPN password and needs it to be changed to something of the social engineer's choosing.
Prerequisites	• Most effective on a mid-sized to large organization where Help Desk personnel are not likely to have a personal rapport with

	all staff members • Knowledge of legitimate user details (name, email address, title, department, gender) • Knowledge of the name of at least one company executive • Do not select a manager, executive or ranking user for this pretext • Knowledge of target Help Desk telephone number
Tools & Equipment	• Mobile phone with SpoofCard application
Play	1. Launch SpoofCard app or mechanism with similar functionality 2. Use the voice change feature and select a gender appropriate voice or simply alter your natural voice 3. Configure spoofed phone number and the dial Help Desk number 4. Be sure to place the call using phony background noise (outside, airport) or place the call outside near busy traffic. 5. Relay the pretext to the target

	6. Play your character out to be a non-technically savvy person. Speak slowly and ask the target to repeat him/herself often. Do this especially in situations where the target attempts to authenticate who you are. Exacerbate by faking a bad phone connection. This will press on the target's patience. 7. Create a sense of urgency. Indicate that an important email or file needs to be sent in the next few minutes and the password needs to be reset immediately. 8. Increase the level of urgency by indicating that {company executive} needs this information sent immediately.

Sleight of Hand	
Objective	To assess the targets susceptibility toward performing privileged actions without properly authenticating the user or divulging confidential information
Description	This is an adaptation of a classic telephone pretext. The premise for this pretext involves the social engineer masquerading as a company IT resource. The social engineer telephones the target asking him/her to visit a website in order to add their computer to the new Windows domain that's currently being built. Meanwhile, the social engineer's actual objective is to capture the target's network username and password. Nowadays, users are trained not to give out passwords, even to their own IT staff. So instead of asking for their password outright which could raise suspicion, the social engineer asks the target to visit a "registration" website where he/she must enter their current username and password in order to be added to the new Windows domain. Behind the scenes, the "registration" website is actually a phony SaaS company whereby any data entered (e.g.: credentials) are captured and saved.
Prerequi-	• Most effective on a mid-sized to large organiza-

sites	tion where Help Desk personnel are not likely to have a personal rapport with all staff members • Knowledge of legitimate user details (name, email address, title, department) • Do not select a manager, executive or ranking user for this pretext • Knowledge of target Help Desk or IT resource telephone number
Tools & Equipment	• Mobile phone with SpoofCard application • Phony website purporting to be a website where the user must register their computer to be added to the new Windows domain • See here for cheap web site templates: https://creativemarket.com/templates/websites • A convincing domain name for the website • A web host provider
Play	1. Invent a name for the phony site 2. Register a domain name for your phony website. Optionally, you may elect to the make the domain name a "private" registration. 3. Procure a web-hosting provider (e.g.: Dreamhost) if you do not already have one.

4. Upload the web site template to the hosting provider. Ensure there is an HTML form with functionality present to capture the information user's credentials.

5. Launch SpoofCard app or other mechanism with similar functionality

6. Use the voice change feature and select a gender appropriate voice or simply alter your natural voice

7. Configure spoofed phone number and the target number

8. Be sure to place the call using phony office background noise. This may be helpful: https://www.youtube.com/watch?v=D7ZZp8XuUTE

9. Telephone the target. Adapt this sample pretext to better fit your target:

   "Hello, [target name], my name is [IT staff name] and we are calling everyone to help coordinate a new IT project. We will be using a service by [phony SaaS] to help us migrate our users to a brand new Windows domain. Before we can begin the migration, we need to have all of our users go to register their systems first. So, I just need you to complete a couple of quick steps.

	Open your browser and go to [phony SaaS website]. Please fill out the form to register your computer." 10. It is recommended that calls to the targets be placed just before the lunch hour or during busy periods. This increases the odds for compliance. Reason being, an unusual request like this may be buried between tasks they have going on at the time and simply forget about it later. It provides less time for the target to stop and question their management about the legitimacy of the request. Lastly, targets will likely either want to complete the request quickly in order to go to lunch or move on with their other tasks.

Financial Foray	
Objective	To assess the targets susceptibility toward performing privileged actions without properly authenticating the user or divulging confidential information
Descrip-tion	In this maneuver, the social engineer telephones the organization's financial department while purporting to be a representative from their banking institution. The goal is to gather sensitive financial information from the target regarding the target company. The type of information sought out should be adapted to fit your pretext. For the purposes of this pretext, the objective is to obtain at least one of the organization's bank account numbers. Again, in order to be valuable, the type of information sought out should be adapted to fit your particular pretext. To effectively carry out this pretext, we should first identify at least one of the organization's banking institutions. Alternatively, a social engineer could assume one of the big name banks by guessing. However, this is recommended only as a last resort. Identifying which bank the target banks with can be obtained through dumpster diving and through other information gathering means. Additionally, the target will automatically expect the

	bank representative (social engineer) to already know some privileged information about them. To substantiate this illusion and to preempt any suspicion by the target, the social engineer should have as much company specific information as possible. For the purposes of this pretext, we will use the organization's IRS Employer Tax ID and their business filing information with their state. This information is public, but can be used to substantiate the illusion of authority and already having privileged information. This information should be used by the social engineer very early in the phone call in order to thwart any suspicion on behalf of the target.
Prerequisites	• Knowledge of the target organization's banking institution (Recommended) • Knowledge of the name of at least one finance/account contact at the target organization
Tools & Equipment	• Mobile phone with SpoofCard application • The Federal EDGAR system: https://searchwww.sec.gov/EDGARFSClient/jsp/EDGAR_MainAccess.jsp • The organization's secretary of state business filings search. Such as: http://mblsportal.sos.state.mn.us/Business/Search

Play	1. Launch SpoofCard app or mechanism with similar functionality 2. Use the voice change feature to alter your natural voice 3. Configure spoofed phone number and the dial financial/accounting target's number 4. Be sure to place the call using phony office background noise. This may be helpful: https://www.youtube.com/watch?v=D7ZZp8XuUTE 5. Telephone the target and adapt this sample pretext to better fit your scenario: "Hello, my name is [fake name] from [organization's bank]. The reason for my call is to validate some information we have in our system in order to resolve a minor issue. The Federal ID we have in the system for [target organization] is [state ID], business type of [i.e.: LLC, S-Corp, etc.] with the mailing address of [address]. Now, my system shows an account number ending in 1000, but has been flagged as invalidated. Could you give me the account number you have associated with [organization's bank] so that I can verify this information and resolve the issue?" 6. If the target complies with the request, I recommend telling the target the situation has

	been resolved instead of leaving the issue open ended. 7. If possible, it is recommended that a female carry out this pretext. Alternatively, it may be possible to use a voice changer that can convincingly alter a male voice to sound like a female.

Attack of the Phones	
Objective	To assess the targets susceptibility toward divulging confidential information
Description	In this pretext, the social engineer attempts to gain sensitive information from the target by purporting to be an automated call from the Internal Revenue Service. The social engineer uses a text-to-speech program to "speak" to the target asking him/her to wait for a representative. Then the target is asked to validate their identity by entering their social security number in by keypad. Meanwhile, the numbers are recorded by the social engineering that will then decode them using a DTMF decoder. While this pretext uses the IRS as its pretext and social security number as its objective, these attributes can be adapted to better compromise the target.
Prerequisites	• Knowledge of the target's phone number
Tools & Equipment	• Mobile phone with SpoofCard application • Recording device to capture the target's social security number

	• Playback device to play the text-to-speech recordings • DTMF decoder, such as: http://dialabc.com/sound/detect/ • Text-to-speech program, such as: http://www.readspeaker.com/voice-demo/
Play	1. Use a text-to-speech program to speak the following text (see ReadSpeaker). Then use a recording device to capture the audio (e.g.: computer's mic). "Hello, this is an automated call from the Internal Revenue Service regarding your [year] income taxes. Please hold for an IRS representative, who will be with you momentarily. For security purposes, please enter your social security number, followed by the pound or hash sign." 2. Once the audio pretext has been captured, ensure that it can be played back during the pretext call 3. Ready the recording device. By having your phone in speakerphone mode, a computer's microphone should be sufficient enough to record the target's social security number 4. Queue the audio pretext for playback

	5. Launch SpoofCard app or mechanism with similar functionality 6. Spoof your phone's outgoing phone number and call the target 7. Set the recording device to record 8. When the target answers, play the audio pretext 9. Hang up after the target enters their social security number 10. If using the suggested DTMF decoder (http://dialabc.com/sound/detect/), you must save the recording as a WAV audio file and upload it to the site to decode the tones

Car Tow	
Objective	To assess the targets susceptibility toward divulging confidential information
Description	In this pretext, the social engineer attempts to gain information about a target by pretending to be a representative from a vehicle towing company. The social engineer convinces the target he/she is towing the vehicle because the target parked in an area where the city is performing construction that day. The car must be towed in order for the city to perform the work and the typical towing fee is $225. In order to gain the target's information, the social engineer provides an alternative to the costly towing fee. The social engineer's alternative is to move the target's vehicle to the next parking stall for only $14. In doing so, the social engineer creates a sense of urgency by indicating the vehicle is already in the lift and the target must make a decision immediately whether he/she wants to be moved to the next stall. To be moved, the target must give the towing company representative a credit card number to process or the vehicle will be impounded.
Prerequi-	• Most effective on a target whose working at a

sites	location where the target's vehicle is not within close proximity to the victim (parking ramp) • Knowledge of the target's phone number • Knowledge of the vehicle's color, make and model
Tools & Equipment	• Mobile phone with SpoofCard application
Play	1. Launch SpoofCard app or mechanism with similar functionality 2. Use the voice change feature and select a gender appropriate voice or simply alter your natural voice 3. Be sure to place the call using phony office background noise. This may be helpful: https://www.youtube.com/watch?v=D7ZZp8XuUTE 4. Telephone the target and adapt this sample pretext to better fit your scenario: "This is [fake towing company name]. Do you own a [vehicle color] [vehicle make and model]?" [Target responds]

"[Ma'am/Sir], you are parked in a stall that has been reserved for minor construction by the city. Our truck has your vehicle up on the lift, but since the stall next to yours is open, we can have our truck move your vehicle over instead of impounding it today. All I need is [very low dollar amount] by credit card."

[Target responds]

5. Speak with an unsympathetic attitude, authoritative tone and a monotone voice. However, don't be rude.

6. The target will likely be upset and may complain about the absence of a posted sign. Simply state that a sign was posted and re-iterate the alternative offer.

7. Do not allow the target to consume too much time on the phone. He/she may be on their way to the location on foot. Be short with answers.

8. Be very brief with verbal communication and re-iterate the low cost alternative. But, do not oversell the alternative. For a more convincing pretext, play it as if you don't care if the target's vehicle is impounded.

9. If the target complies with your request, indicate the situation has been resolved and end the call swiftly. Hanging up immediately after receiving

	the information will raise immediate suspicion.

Baiting

Baiting, or media baiting, involves the attacker "baiting" a target into using a piece of malware-infected media by piquing the target's curiosity into inserting it into their computer. Typically, the infected media would covertly launch a malicious program unbeknownst to the user, once he or she inserts the media into their computer.

Oldie but A Goody	
Objective	To assess the targets susceptibility toward inserting untrusted media into their computers
Description	This is a classic baiting maneuver. In this maneuver, the social engineer would infect several USB drives configured to launch a malicious program when inserted into a computer. SET is used to create an infected Metasploit payload and autorun.inf designed to connect back to a listener.
Prerequisites	• Knowledge of the physical location(s) • Close physical proximity to the target location(s)
Tools &	• Several U3 USB flash drives

Equipment	• Social Engineer Toolkit (SET) • Metasploit Framework
Play	1. Launch SET, select *Infectious Media Generator* from the main menu, then select *Standard Metasploit Executable* 2. SET will create a PDF payload and autorun file. Copy the contents of the folder to a CD/DVD/USB to autorun. 3. Start the listener using your publicly available IP address and preferred port 4. Label the USB drives with the following labels, "Private Pics," "Payroll," and "Beach Pics, Videos" 5. Leave the USB drives at the target location near public doors, parking lot, walkways closest to the target. 6. Monitor for results and wait for targets to connect.

Blazing Fast Interwebs	
Objective	To assess the targets susceptibility toward inserting untrusted media into their computers
Description	In this maneuver, the social engineer would infect one or more USB drives configured to launch a malicious program when inserted into a computer. SET is used to create an infected Metasploit payload and autorun.inf designed to connect back to a listener. The infected drive will be mailed to the target under the false pretenses it is a company marketing campaign.
Prerequisites	• Knowledge of the target(s) mailing address(es)
Tools & Equipment	• One or more U3 USB flash drives • Social Engineer Toolkit (SET) • Metasploit Framework • Microsoft Word or Photoshop
Play	1. Launch SET, select *Infectious Media Generator* from the main menu, then select

	Standard Metasploit Executable 2. SET will create a PDF payload and autorun file. Copy the contents of the folder to a CD/DVD/USB to autorun. 3. Start the listener using your publicly available IP address and preferred port 4. Create an advertisement flyer to be included in the mailing. The flyer must entice the target into plugging in the USB device. 5. Utilize the following pretext: a. **Amazing Internet Accelerator Device:** This is a promotional flyer purporting to be a major Internet provider (e.g., Comcast) or Google that introduces "innovative" technology that triples Internet speeds by way of technology on the enclosed USB device. Free of charge and no setup required; simply connect and go. Microsoft Templates Online could be used to design a promo flyer for the phony product. 6. Mail the infected USB drives. 7. Monitor for results and wait for targets to connect.

Save Big Money!	
Objective	To assess the targets susceptibility to inserting untrusted media into their computers
Description	In this maneuver, the social engineer would infect one or more USB drives configured to launch a malicious program when inserted into a computer. SET is used to create an infected Metasploit payload and autorun.inf designed to connect back to a listener. The infected drive will be mailed to the target under the false pretenses it is a company marketing campaign.
Prerequisites	• Knowledge of the target(s) mailing address(es)
Tools & Equipment	• One or more U3 USB flash drives • Social Engineer Toolkit (SET) • Metasploit Framework • Microsoft Word or Photoshop

<table>
<tr>
<td>Play</td>
<td>
1. Launch SET, select Infectious Media Generator from the main menu, then select Standard Metasploit Executable

2. SET will create a PDF payload and autorun file. Copy the contents of the folder to a CD/DVD/USB to autorun.

3. Start the listener using your publicly available IP address and preferred port

4. Create an advertisement flyer to be included in the mailing. The flyer must entice the target into plugging in the USB device.

5. Utilize the following pretext:

Coupon book on USB: a promotional flyer would be developed to masquerade as a company who delivers free coupon books for big box stores (Target, Best Buy, Wal-Mart, Cabella's, Sears) via USB drives. The flyer should promise sensational savings of over 50% off. Microsoft Templates Online could be used to design a promo flyer for the phony product.

8. Mail the infected USB drives.

9. Monitor for results and wait for targets to connect.
</td>
</tr>
</table>

Recalling All Cars!	
Objective	To assess the targets susceptibility toward inserting untrusted media into their computers
Description	In this maneuver, the social engineer would infect one or more USB drives configured to launch a malicious program when inserted into a computer. SET is used to create an infected Metasploit payload and autorun.inf designed to connect back to a listener. The infected drive will be mailed to the target under the false pretense that the target's vehicle requires a grave recall needing immediate attention.
Prerequisites	• Requires knowledge of the make/model of the target vehicle. This can be obtained through surveillance of the target or via online intelligence gathering techniques (Maltego, Social Media). • Optionally, if the target's vehicle make/model are unknown, the content of the formal business letter could be made to generically reference the vehicle without

	specifying this information. • Requires knowledge of the target's mailing address
Tools & Equipment	• U3 USB flash drive • Social Engineer Toolkit (SET) • Metasploit Framework • Microsoft Word or Photoshop
Play	1. Launch SET, select *Infectious Media Generator* from the main menu, then select *Standard Metasploit Executable* 2. SET will create a PDF payload and autorun file. Copy the contents of the folder to a CD/DVD/USB to autorun. 3. Start the listener using your publicly available IP address and preferred port 4. Create a formal business letter to be included in the recall mailing. The letter must entice the target into plugging in the USB device in order to obtain critical information for the processing of his/her vehicle's recall. 5. Use and adapt the following content for the

	recall letter *Dear Customer,* *This notice is sent to you in accordance with the requirements of the National Traffic and Motor Vehicle Safety Act.* *[Company name] has decided that a defect, which relates to motor vehicle safety, requires immediate replacement. Therefore, please follow the instructions below.* *1). Plug in the enclosed USB drive into your computer.* *2). Navigate to the USB drive and open the PDF file titled [PDF file name].* *3). Read and print the recall form.* *4). Sign the form and mail it using the enclosed pre-addressed postage ready envelope.* *We apologize for this situation and want to assure you that, with your assistance, we aim to remedy this condition immediately. Our commitment, together with your dealer, is to provide you with the highest level of service and we stand by that commitment.*

	At [company name], we genuinely care about quality and the safety of our customers. 6. Mail the infected USB drive to the target along with the formal business letter. 7. Monitor results and wait for the target to connect.

Bank Security Software	
Objective	To assess the target's susceptibility toward inserting untrusted media into their computers
Description	This is a media baiting adaptation of the spear phishing pretext called, "Bank Security Email Alert." In this maneuver, the social engineer would infect one or more USB drives configured to launch a malicious program when inserted into a computer. SET is used to create an infected Metasploit payload and autorun.inf designed to connect back to a listener. The infected drive will be mailed to the targets under the false pretenses their bank has noticed suspicious activity on the target account. And the enclosed USB drive contains secure software to disinfect their computer and ensure secure connectivity to the bank website.
Prerequisites	• Knowledge of the target email address • Knowledge of the target's bank. This may be learned through surveillance, dumpster diving or GPS tracking.

Tools & Equipment	• One or more U3 USB flash drives • Social Engineer Toolkit (SET) • Metasploit Framework • Microsoft Word or Photoshop
Play	1. Launch SET, select *Social Engineering Attacks -> Spear-Phishing Attack Vector ->* then select *Perform a Mass Email Attack* 2. Select *Adobe PDF Embedded EXE Social Engineering* and opt for the built-in BLANK PDF, then select the *Windows Reverse TCP Shell.* 3. Enter your IP address for the payload listener and the listening port (443) 4. Create a formal business letter to be included in the recall mailing. The letter must entice the target into plugging in the USB device in order to obtain critical information about the suspicious activity and the security software. 5. Use the following text: *Dear Customer* *You are receiving this message because you are a current [bank name] customer.*

Our Fraud & Prevention department has detected several suspicious transactions on your account originating from multiple overseas merchants. These charges Our policy states that we require your assistance in determining the legitimacy of any suspicious charges totaling over $10,000. Your cooperation is appreciated.

To ensure your computer is protected and to facilitate secure connectivity to the Internet, please follow the instructions below.

1). Plug the enclosed USB drive into your computer.

2). Navigate to the USB drive and open the PDF file titled [PDF file name].

3). Review each suspicious transaction shown along with the merchant, date and transaction amount.

4). Observe and note any transactions as suspicious charges to the best of your ability.

5). Instructions regarding how to download our secure software are included on the final page.

Your information is very important to us.

	We appreciate your cooperation. A representative will be contacting you shortly regarding this matter. Please reference incident number: FRDR-2039423990 6. Mail the infected USB drive to the target along with the formal business letter. 7. Monitor results and wait for the target to connect.

Introducing NLP: Psychological Skills for Understanding and Influencing People (Neuro-Linguistic Programming), by Joseph O'Connor

Social Engineering: The Art of Human Hacking, by Christopher Hadnagy

Resources

RedTeam Security http://www.redteamsecure.com/

BrickHouse Security http://www.brickhousesecurity.com/

Research Projects http://www.redteamsecure.com/labs/all_projects

LinkedIn http://www.linkedin.com/in/jtalamantes/

Facebook http://www.facebook.com/redteamsecure

Twitter http://twitter.com/redteamsecure

Printed in Great Britain
by Amazon

47373386R00119